Erotic Art 2

Erotic Art 2

Compiled by

Drs. Phyllis and Eberhard Kronhausen

GROVE PRESS, INC., NEW YORK

ACKNOWLEDGMENTS

We should like to thank the Galérie Louise Leiris, Paris, for the works of André Masson and Pablo Picasso; the Galérie A. F. Petit, Paris, for Hans Bellmer and Salvador Dali; the National Museum, Stockholm, for Johan Tobias Sergel and Carl August Ehrensvärd; and the David Stuart Galleries, Los Angeles, for one of the George Grosz watercolors. We should like to express our appreciation for the help of Manuel Gonzalez of the Sidney Janis Gallery, New York, Michael Findlay of the Richard Feigen Gallery, New York, and for the photography of Jay Good, Geoffrey Clements, and Dan Lenore. Thanks also to Tiemen Ottink of Quick Agentschap NV, Holland, for his careful supervision of the negative work in this volume, and to Mark Cieply, Emilio Elias, Barbara Hirsch, Sue Gillson, Nonoy Marcelo, Anda Pirvics, Rusty Porter (who supervised the manufacture), Diane Robbins (for the Index), Ruth Ross, Harry Rowohlt, and Stephanie Tevonian. Our especial thanks to Michael Perpich, our designer, and to Arnold Leo, our editor, for the energy expended in bringing this volume together.

Library of Congress Catalog Card Number: 68-57504

First Printing

Designed by Michael W. Perpich

Manufactured in the United States of America

CONTENTS

FOREWORD

The era of pornography is coming to an end, for pornography is possible only where censorship exists. The repressive manners of Victorian England, which produced more "hard-core" smut than any other period in Western history, may still linger with us. But contemporary society is reluctantly becoming more tolerant toward sexuality. Thus, pornography as we know it—the tawdry, though often highly overpriced sex trash in the form of books or pictures that are offered "under the counter"—is, happily, on the way out. Like bootleg whisky, smut becomes something else when legalized.

In the open market, the process of supply and demand assures a competitive price level, as long as advertising does not induce customers to buy what they don't want at prices they can't afford. When a product is put on sale in the open, the customer not only gets a lower price, he has an opportunity to choose the best and reject the worst. Few people will accept tawdry products when they can have beautiful ones, and so erotic art and writing become progressively more removed from the low-brow prototypes. The writing, the photography, the drawing, or whatever the medium of communication may be, becomes more artistic, is done in much better taste, and is manufactured with greater care. In other words, the works gradually move to a higher esthetic and intellectual level, and even the print and paper used in the production of the new erotica has improved dramatically wherever censorship has been eliminated. In Denmark and Sweden this is true to such a degree that these countries may point the way to the rest of the world as they once did with modern furniture and household design. Their lead in this field has been proven time and again: Sweden was first to allow The First International Exhibition of Erotic Art, in 1968, while Denmark was first to hold an open trade fair of the new pornography entrepreneurs, in 1969.

Pornography, in the legal meaning of the term—and there really is no other meaningful distinction between pornographic and nonpornographic art or literature—is utterly without "redeeming social value." In the visual arts, such as painting, sculpture, graphics, and photography, we understand by "redeeming social value" a concern on the part of the artist with composition, color, light, movement, texture—in short, a concern with art (but this is not necessarily the only or "official" meaning of the legal terminology, which is vague and open to multiple interpretation). In literature, drama, and the cinema, similar artistic criteria prevail, but in these media the presence of an idea, a philosophy of life, or a personal point of view on the part of the author or film-maker may be of more importance than in the nonliterary arts. It logically follows that the more a pictorial or literary work shows evidence of these artistic and intellectual criteria, the more it is removed from the official definition of pornography.

In Sweden and Denmark, where censorship has been recognized as undemocratic, as well as ineffectual, pornography (in the old, under-the-counter sense of the term) has begun to disappear. True, a good deal of the old stuff is still around, and it will continue to be produced as long as there are large, lucrative black markets available in the bordering censorship countries and as long as the tourist demand persists. But it is now virtually impossible for dealers to sell sloppy and thoughtless junk to the native population which, in a very short time after the abolition of censorship, became too sophisticated to absorb these low-quality erotic products that might be funny but are also a sad mirror of the low esteem in which society still holds the physical aspects of sexual relations.

Along with the highly improved techniques of producing erotica, there is a new interest among artists in Sweden, Denmark, and to an ever increasing extent also in America and elsewhere, to experiment with sexual subject matter. The concern of this movement in the arts is not so much with mere sexual stimulation—the competition from still photography and movie camera is far too great for that—as with sexual fantasies, the expression of socially critical ideas, or simply with the artistic possibilities inherent in the hitherto neglected area of sexuality. Even in the prephotographic past, such artistic and intellectual concerns have played a large part in the production of erotic art. Religious concepts and sentiments, for example, frequently motivated its production, as in India, Tibet, Nepal, primitive Africa, South America, and Polynesia. But erotic art frequently also served, quite unblushingly, as a stimulus to erotic fantasies, that is, as a psychological aphrodisiac, as in the secular erotic art of India, China, and Japan, as well as in the West.

In the erotic art of Japan and China, deliberate erotic appeal often went hand in hand with educational motivations. Japanese and Chinese erotic picture scrolls were frequently given to young brides to instruct them in the arts of physical love (presumably, the young bridegroom had already received this education through repeated visits to the "pleasure quarters"). Aside from the educational aspect of Chinese and Japanese erotic art, the picture scrolls and fine prints were treasured by connoisseurs for their artistic merits, either for the personal delight of the individual collector or for the entertainment of suitable (male) guests for whom a precious scroll might be displayed in the course of civilized social intercourse between persons of good taste and with an appreciation for the finer things of life.

The West has no similar tradition, at least not on such a large scale. One might say that at certain periods, such as the Renaissance in Italy or the eighteenth century in France, erotic art was appreciated by a portion of the upper class as part of a gracious style of living. But this appreciation by a small group of wealthy and well-educated art lovers in Europe cannot really be equated with the wide-spread acceptance of erotica in the East. There, especially in seventeenth- and eighteenth-century Japan, a broad, well-to-do middle class collected and enjoyed fine erotic art. Consequently, Japan (and, to a lesser extent, China and India) produced the finest and most varied erotic art we know.

In our own period in the history of human civilization, erotic art takes on special significance: with the very real threat of racial extinction through sheer overpopulation, the procreative possibilities of sex are becoming an undesirable by-product —rather than the moral justification—of sexual relations. However, if modern men and women learn to appreciate sex for recreation rather than procreation, civilization as we know it may survive. The meaning of erotic art, if it has a message at all, is just that: it reminds us vividly and convincingly that, contrary to what most sex education seems to stress, sex is not to make babies, but for the enjoyment of the senses, for emotional catharsis, for physical and mental release, for giving and receiving of pleasure, for the sharing of physical and emotional experience, for lightening the burdens of the day and the forgetting of tomorrow. And there is nothing like erotic art to portray all the diverse aspects of human sexuality and to do it in a never-ending flow of imaginative forms that enrich our lives and help us understand ourselves at a profound level.

This, then, is the true function of erotic art. It also explains why humor is such a vital aspect of it: there is a decidedly funny side to sex, and both Eastern and Western artists have amply provided for comic relief when dealing with sexual subject matter.

Sometimes this erotic humor has, in turn, a serious side to it, as humor in general often has. In the eighteenth and nineteenth centuries, erotic humor became the vehicle for political, social, and religious dissent, especially in the form of easily reproduced lithographs. Contemporary artists also use erotic humor for the same purposes. Ungerer, Rahmberg, and Félicien Rops may be cited as examples from this volume (see Index). Other artists have used subtler but no less devastating means to express social protest. Bellmer's brooding, obsessional sensuality, for instance, should not detract from the fact that he is deliberately shocking bourgeois sensibilities. It is almost as if Bellmer had spent a lifetime in perfecting an absolutely superior graphic style, only to frustrate the bourgeois collector by using his envied craft entirely for the portrayal of socially unacceptable subject matter.

A similar case in point is George Grosz. He put virtually all his art in the service of social criticism, and thus distinguished himself by gaining the deep enmity of the Nazis, which ultimately forced him to leave his native Germany. In a way, perhaps, all erotic art is a form of social protest, as long as society tolerates and even fosters moral hypocrisy, as long as it engages in the suppression of normal, healthy sexuality, and as long as it censors the free expression of erotic subject matter in literature, the arts, and the cinema. But it is equally true that erotic art frequently represents the most subjective, the most intimate, and the psychologically most profound part of an artist's work. These are the two supplementary aspects of erotic art that combine to give it its unique position in the representational arts.

On this subjective, individual level, erotic art is the medium par excellence for the representation and externalization of sexual fantasies, e.g., Bellmer's nubile young girls, his interchangeable female anatomy, his sharp focus on the male and female sex organs, alone or combined, with or without copulation, his curious though not infrequent juxtaposition of death and eroticism, and his already mentioned deliberate search for the shocking and obscene.

One could go on analyzing each artist in this collection, but we would rather stop here. After all, each work offers more than one possibility of interpretation. For our part, we have included in *Erotic Art 1* and *Erotic Art 2* all those pieces of definite artistic merit which in some way contribute to the wide subject of sexuality. We have tried to set aside our own tastes and esthetic preferences to ensure the widest possible coverage of relevant subject matter. In this way, we hope we have presented a true sampling of erotic art from historical, cross-cultural, and individual points of view.

Some readers will no doubt regret the lack of classical Greek, Etruscan, and Roman art. The reason for this omission is not only that we do not at present own any examples from those periods, but that a great deal of classical work has been published over the years, both in Europe and in America, e.g., the publications of Edward Fuchs in Germany, dating from 1910–20, the four-volume *Bilder-Lexikon der Erotik* from the 1920's (recently reissued in Germany with two supplementary volumes), the contemporary Lo Duca series of publications in France (Société des Editions Jean-Jacques Pauvert, Paris), and various other publications in Europe and America.

In our writings, and lately also through the medium of the motion picture,* we have always expressed our strong conviction that sexuality, whether expressed by direct action or indirectly by artistic or literary productions, needs no "socially redeeming value" to justify its existence. This is so, in our opinion, because sexuality is not the dangerous antisocial bugaboo that Western society has unfortunately come to regard it.

If one examines the roots from which this strange notion about the alleged dangers of sexuality has sprung, one discovers that they reach deeply into our Judeo-Christian heritage. Not that the mainstream of Judaism—of which Christianity is, after all, an offshoot—is fundamentally opposed to sexuality. On the contrary, the Old Testament testifies to a rather permissive attitude toward sexuality. The only critical comments about sexual behavior in the Old Testament are to be found in the pronouncements of some of the prophets who were warning more against the sexual excesses of the ruling classes (i.e., a social evil) than against sexuality itself. But there also existed at certain Biblical times a fanatically ascetic undercurrent in the Jewish religion (just as it exists in the Islamic and Buddhist traditions as well) which condemned all forms of sensuality and which looked upon the pursuit of sexual pleasure as the prime enemy of spirituality. In this respect, Hinduism has been much more realistic psychologically. It holds that a person can ultimately overcome the world of the senses only by first exercising and embracing them without reservation, in other words, without the mechanism of repression and the setting up of artificial taboos and avoidance patterns.

---

*Freedom to Love, a feature-length documentary relating five cases of legal interference with the private sex lives of people, including the case of a fifteen-year-old girl, said to be a minor, and a twenty-five-year-old male; a lesbian couple; a case involving abortion; the case of a psychologist who used a call girl as a therapeutic adjunct for a male patient with potency disturbance; and a group-sex case. The cases are supplemented and supported by interviews with scientists and prominent personalities, as well as by excerpts from erotic theater plays and The Second International Exhibition of Erotic Art in Stockholm, 1969.

The ascetic trend in Judaism flowered in the teachings of John the Baptist and Jesus of Nazareth (seat of the ascetic sect of Nazarenes). However, the historical Jesus, though apparently disinterested in sex, seems to have been quite tolerant toward sexuality (witness his behavior at the wedding in Canaan, his open acceptance of Mary Magdalene, etc.). In fact, up to this point, Judeo-Christian thought is no more antisexual or antisensual than, say, Buddhism, which also advocates the overcoming of the "illusory world of the senses" and which holds that the absence of all desire will lead to the ideal mental state, to be attained, however, only by the few truly enlightened ones, or Buddhas.

After the execution of Jesus, his followers split from the Jewish faith and quite another situation developed. The morbid antisexualism of the Apostle Paul needs no elaboration. He was soon followed by other early Church leaders who suffered from similar obsessional guilt complexes and who never tired of exhorting their followers against the temptations of the flesh. Under this kind of influence, the antisexual tradition of Christianity developed, coming to a bloody climax of reaction formations with the witch hunts and the Inquisition. Woman was by then seen mainly as the temptress, as the one who had first succumbed to the lure of the senses by taking the advice of the serpent in the Garden of Eden and offering her male companion the forbidden fruit.

As the Christian faith became the religion of state, these mysogenistic and antisexual attitudes became the official code of ethics of Western society and the basis of its social institutions and legal structure. It is by this process that the state first became interested in what was happening in the bedrooms of its citizenry. Thus, all official attempts of government to regulate and interfere with the private sex life of the individual and all forms of sexual censorship have their roots in this dark sectarian subsoil, and not in the enlightened visions of Judeo-Christian tradition.

Of course, there is every reason to protect society from sexual sadists, rapists, and child-molesters. One might include certain types of voyeurism and exhibitionism in this category if it involves the invasion of others' privacy. But beyond this, only the unquestioning certainty of those who are hopelessly blinded by religious dogma—and the . particular arrogance which usually accompanies it—could arrogate to themselves the right to proscribe and legislate in an area as private as the individual's way of expressing the strivings of his basic humanity. Thus the official regulation of sexual behavior that is not clearly antisocial and all forms of sexual censorship are due to a continuing failure to truly separate the functions of church and state. This is so even where, as in the United States, the laws specifically provide for such separation—a goal and ideal of democracy which has yet to be fully realized. Meanwhile, a sectarian code of ethics is forced upon each and every member of societies where this separation has not yet been implemented by legal reform in the area of sexuality. As a result, sizable minorities in these societies are forced against their beliefs and volition to abide, as well as they may, by ethical standards other than those which they themselves hold, or at least to arrange their entire public lives to look as if they were abiding by the official moral code.

Instead of this schizoid mentality on the part of most societies, we feel strongly that a natural attitude toward sexuality is infinitely more desirable for mental hygiene than any kind of suppression of the normal, healthy sex drive. Nor do we think that sexual happiness and freedom from unnecessary inhibitions and repressions are necessarily opposed to a religious attitude and reverence for life. Rather, eroticism seems to us to be the base of all true religious feeling. Consequently, young people should enter early into responsible sexual relations, each respecting the partner's personal rights and needs. For the development of sensuality, of the giving and taking of pleasure, and of making contact with another's mind and body through sexuality is infinitely preferable to the deadening of the senses and the kind of emotional isolation which has no other means to establish contact with another living being than by the knife, the fist, or the gun.

And yet governments are tolerating and even promoting the propaganda of death and violence, which emanates daily from every picture tube in millions of living rooms, from the pages of the daily newspaper, the cinema screen, and from countless publications in every language and dialect of the world, while trying to curtail and suppress the propaganda of life-giving Eros. Perhaps underlying such an illogical state of affairs is the intuitive understanding on the part of warlike societies (and what society is not warlike?) that sexual frustration and a tendency toward violence on the part of the citizenry may serve such societies well for the emergency of war. It is therefore possibly no accident that so far the only two nations that have felt secure enough to abandon almost all official suppression of sexuality and all forms of sexual censorship are Denmark and Sweden—both societies with only minor military interests and establishments and strong pacifistic tendencies. Not quite accidentally, these are also countries which enjoy relative freedom from material want and which give their citizenry the greatest measure of economic security yet achieved.

One is led to ask if the official resistance toward sexual freedom and the abolition of sexual censorship are interrelated with certain political and economic realities. If so, the hysterically ruthless suppression of sexual freedom on the part of certain political establishments becomes at once understandable. It also leads one to suspect that progress in the sexual area can only be proportional to progress in these other social and economic areas.

To this political and economic resistance against sexual freedom must be added certain psychological factors of a more personal nature which are no less important. After all, there still exists in Western society a sizable group of people who are trying so hard to be "good" that they feel intensely threatened by any increase in libido that might upset the delicate balance between their sexual needs and their efforts to channel these needs into the only socially approved outlets available to them. They therefore insist vehemently and militantly on the social suppression of sexuality and on the enforcement of censorship out of what they consider to be self-protective interests. It helps little to argue against such irrational fears with logic and scientific proof. Even the large-scale example of Denmark and Sweden, where the crime rate for sexual offenses continues to decline as these societies become more and more permissive, holds little persuasive argument for this group of people.

Yet, in spite of all these obstacles to human progress in general and to progress in the sexual area in particular, we firmly believe that the time has come when advanced societies, like the United States, must take seriously the professed separation of church and state and grant to every citizen the right to work out his or her own moral salvation in accordance with the individual's conscience, with responsibility and in accordance with the true democratic process.

Erotic Art 2

1—*Rembrandt (1606–69), engraving.*

2

2–4—Thomas Rowlandson (1756–1827; England), watercolor.

3

4

Τοιαδ επ' εχθρας τους εμους ελθοι Κυπρις.

5

6

6

Henry Fuseli (1741–1825; Switzerland and England).
5—*Pencil.* **6**—*Pencil and watercolor.*

7

8

8

Giör alla Rätt

9

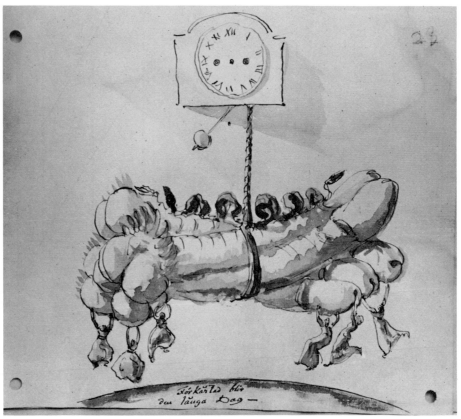

Giör Kärlek blir
den långa Dag —

10

Johan Tobias Sergel (1740–1814; Sweden). **7–9–10—**
Sepia. **8—**Watercolor.

11

Johan Tobias Sergel. **11–12**—*Pencil.* **13**—*Sepia.*

12

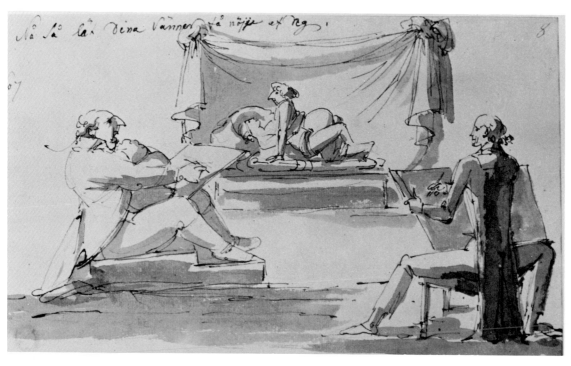

13

11

14

15

14–15—*Frédéric Bouchot (France), from* Diabolico Foutromanie, *a portfolio of illustrations depicting the then popular "Diableries," or "Pranks of the Devils," early 19th century.*

16

17

16–17—*Frédéric Bouchot, from* Diabolico Foutromanie.

18

19

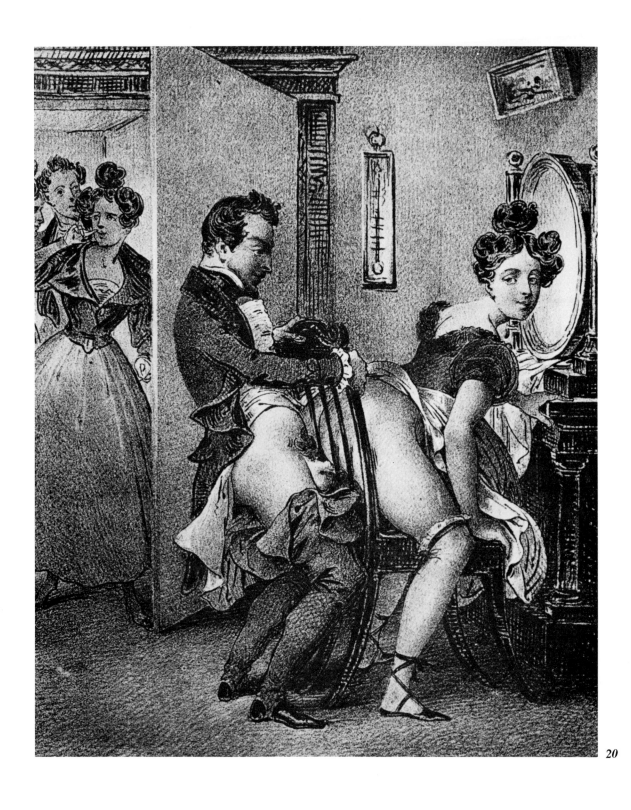

20

18–20—Anonymous French etchings, 19th century.

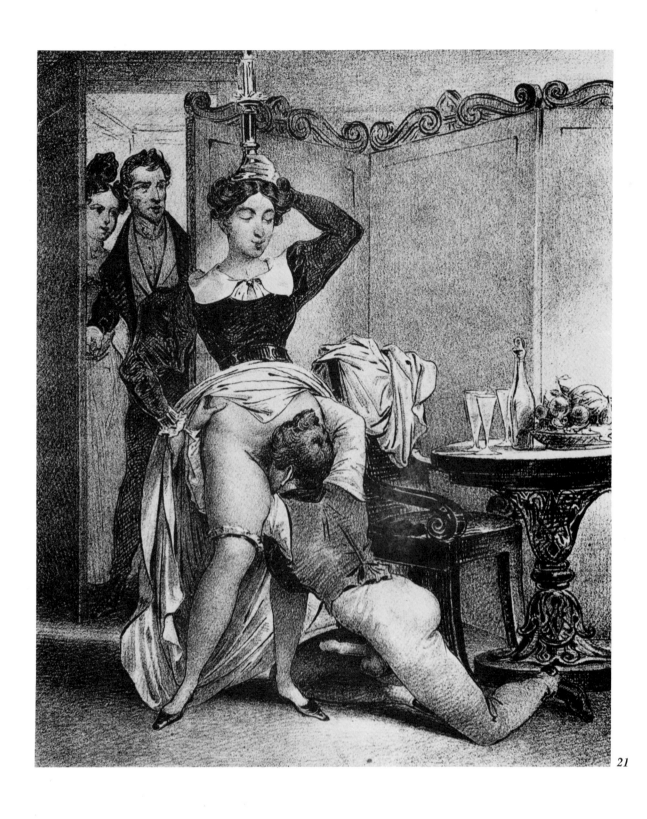

21

21—*Anonymous French etching, 19th century.*
22—*Félicien Rops (1833–98; Belgium), lithograph.*

I-VIII—*George Grosz (Germany and U.S.), watercolors from late 1920's.*

I

III

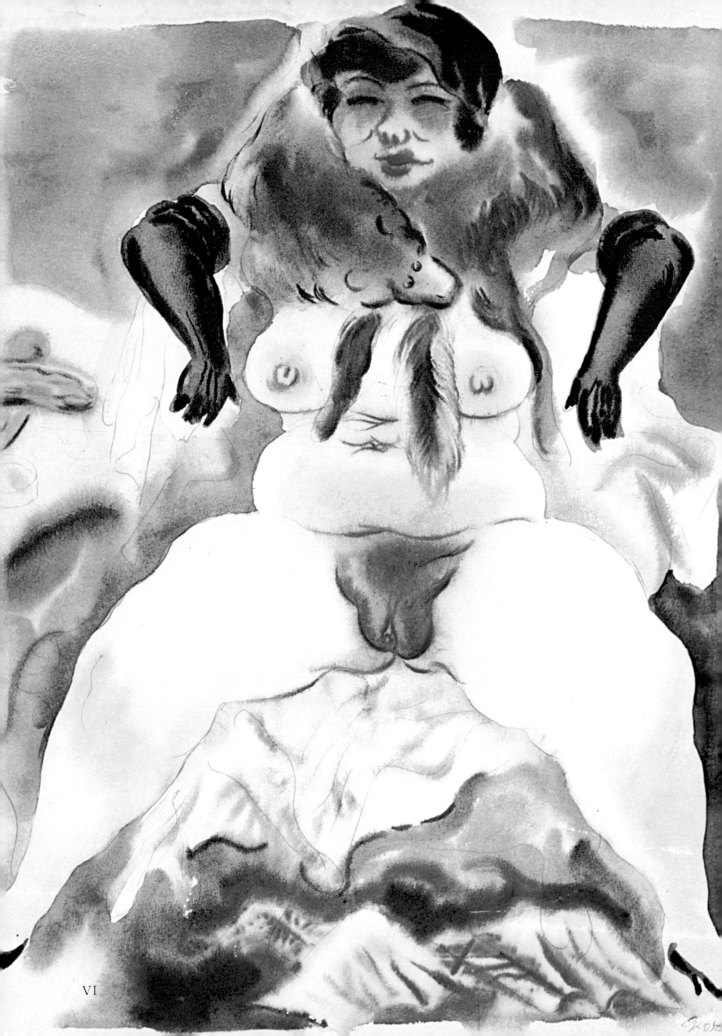

VI

VII

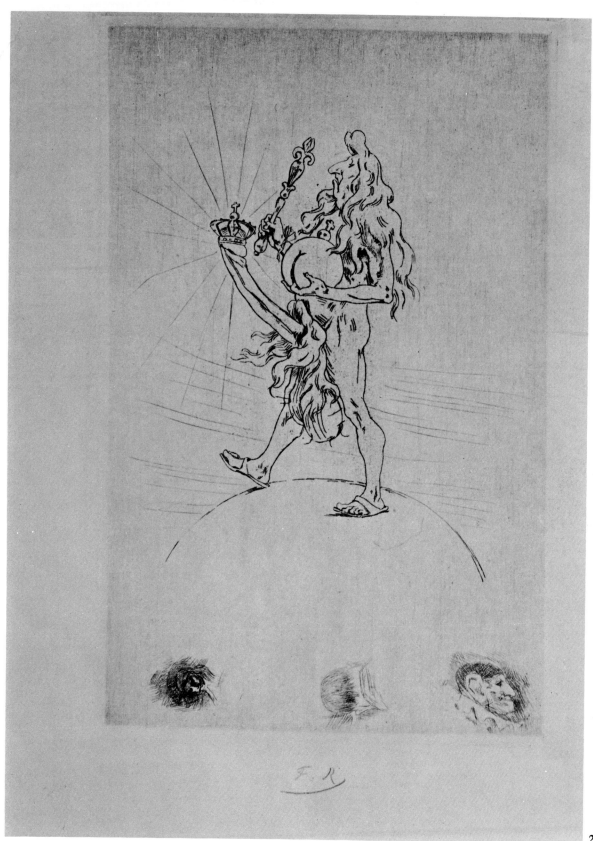

VIII

23

24

20

25

26

*Félicien Rops. 23–24—Lithographs. 25–26—Colored
lithographs.*

TRES INSATURABILIA:
INFERNUS, TERRA ET OS VULVÆ
S. AUGUSTIN   1879

27

28

27–28—*Félicien Rops, lithographs.*

29

*29–31—Franz von Bayros (1866–1942 ; Austria),
lithographs.*

30

31

VISET

32

*32–33—Viset (France), etchings from a series of
humorous book illustrations, ca. 1900.*

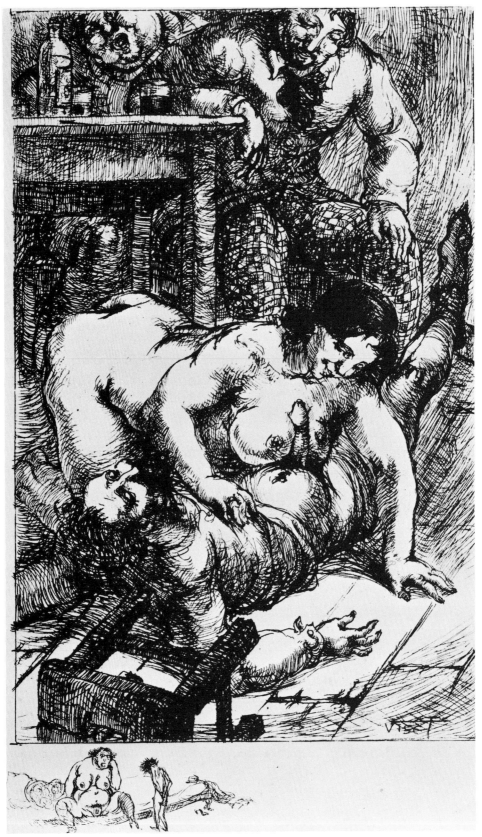

34–35—*Viset, etchings from a series of humorous book illustrations, ca. 1900.*

36

36—Viset, etching from a series of humorous book illustrations, ca. 1900. **37–38—***Nicolaus Vadasz (1884–1927; Hungary and France), drawings.*

37

38

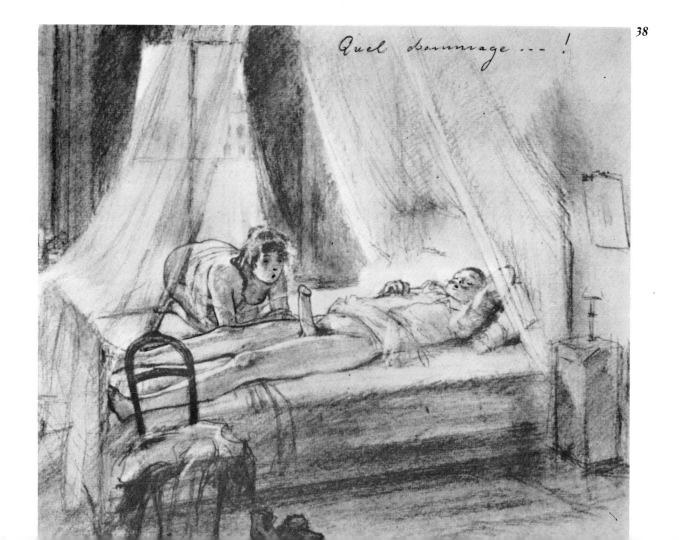

39

40

41

Auguste Rodin (1840–1917; France). **39**—Watercolor.
40—Pencil.
41—Jules Pascin (1885–1930; France), lithograph.

42

43

44

45

42–45—Jules Pascin, lithographs.

46

47

46—Jules Pascin, pencil. 47—Gustav Klimt (1862–1918; Austria), illustration from Hetärengespräche des Lukian *(German edition published by Zeifler, Leipzig, 1907), pencil. 48—Gustav Klimt, pencil. 49—Gustav Klimt, pencil (collection Emilio Greco).*

48

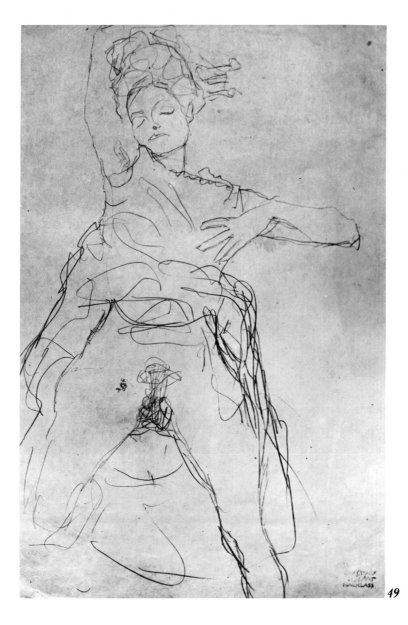

49

8/100

51

50—*Anonymous etching (Germany/Austria?), ca. 1920.*
51—*Michel Fingesten (Germany), ca. 1920.*

52

53

52–55—*Gerda Wegener (1885–1940; Denmark),
watercolors.*

54

55

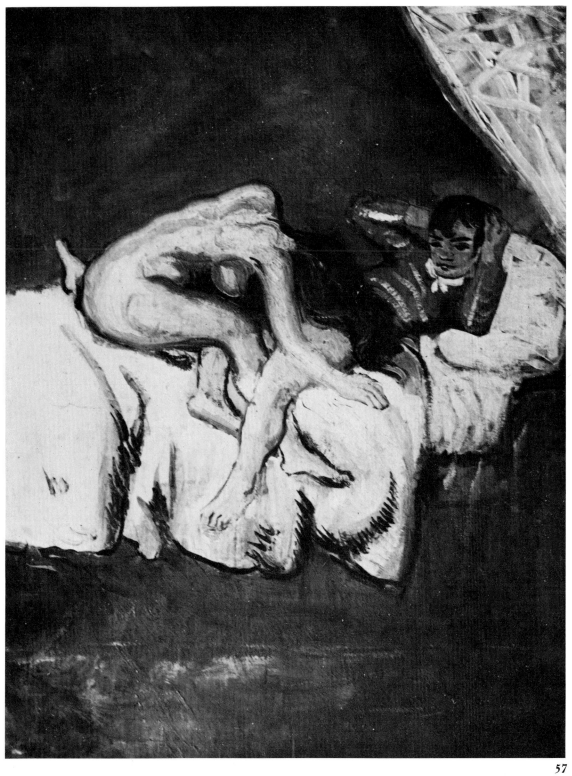

57

56—*George Grosz (Germany and U.S.), watercolor.*
57—*Pablo Picasso (Spain and France), oil painting
(said to be an autobiographical portrait of the artist).*

43

58

Pablo Picasso. **58**—*Etching.* **59–60**—*Lithographs. (The dates on figures* **58–60** *are reversed in the original prints, since the artist dated the plates and not the prints.)*

59

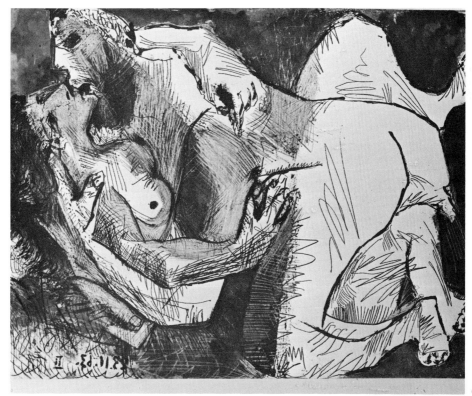

60

61

61—*Pablo Picasso, lithograph.* 62—*Salvador Dali (Spain), pencil.*

63

64

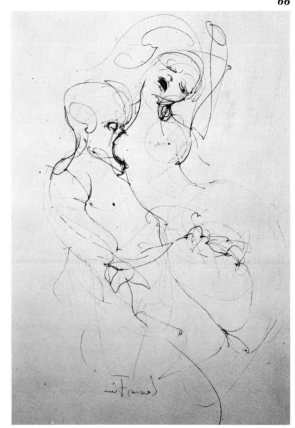

63–67—*Leonor Fini (Trieste and France), drawings.*

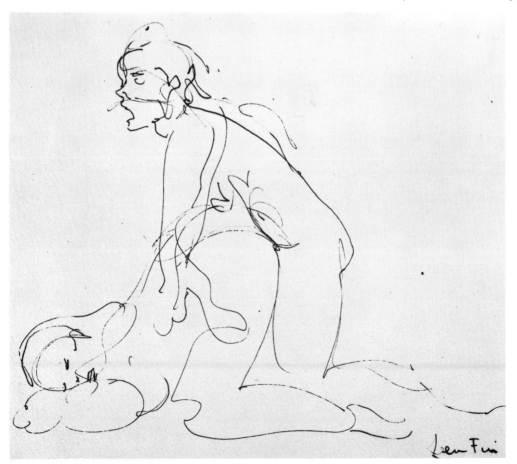

68

André Masson (France). 68—Watercolor. 69—Ink.
70—Colored ink.

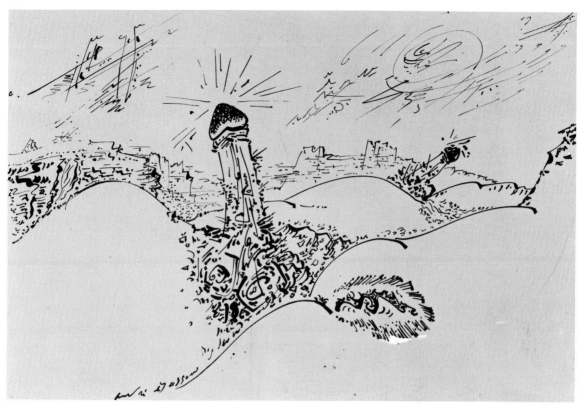

69

70

51

ERÔS
HÔTEL

71

52

1956

72

André Masson. **71**—*Etching.* **72**—*Ink drawing.*

73

74—(inset)

73-75—*Hans Bellmer (Germany and France), pencil.*

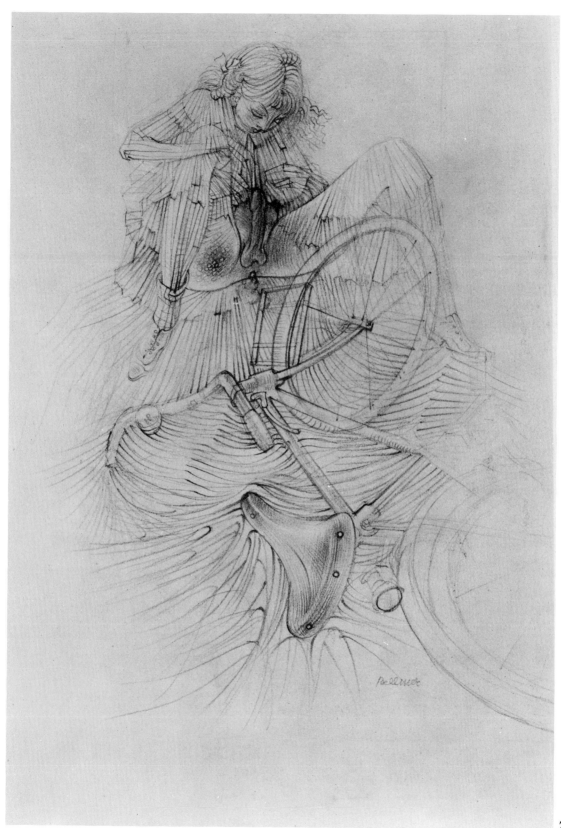

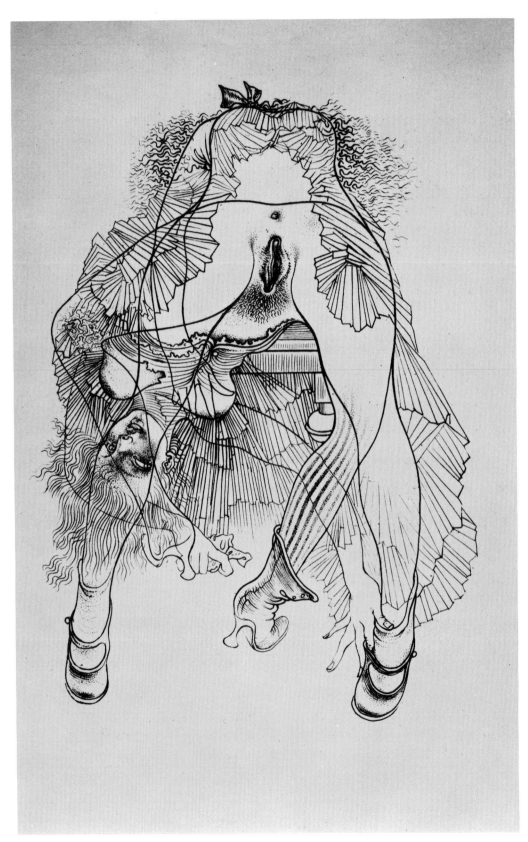

76

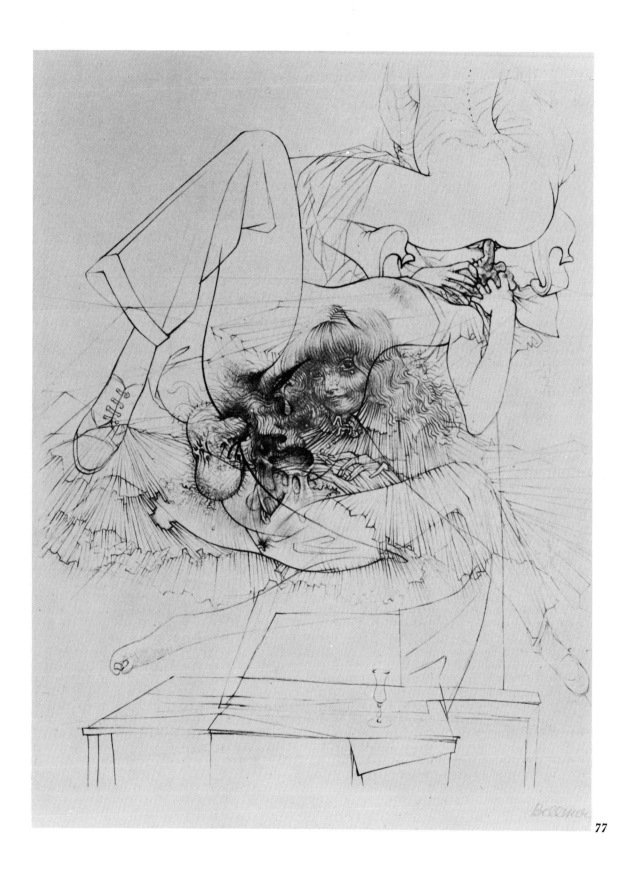

77

Hans Bellmer. **76**—Copper engraving. **77**—Etching.

78

78–79—*Hans Bellmer, etchings.*

80

80-81—Hans Bellmer, *pencil.*

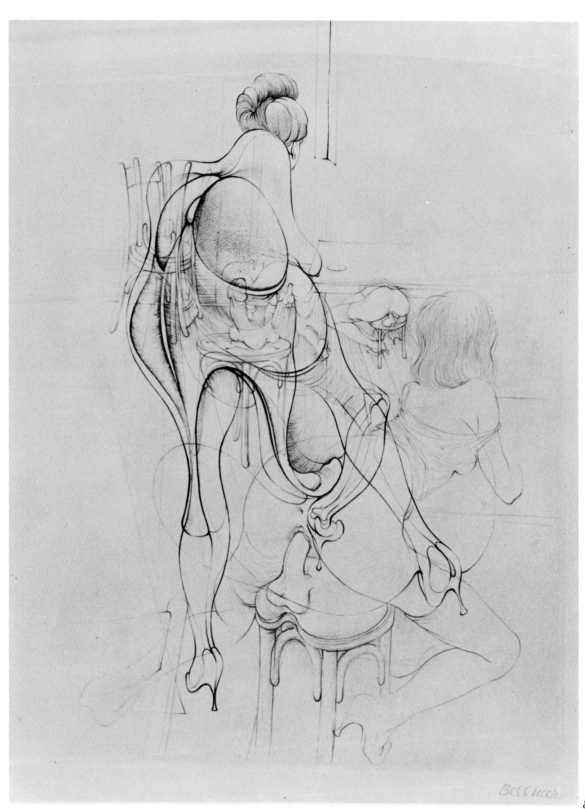

81

63.

82

Hans Bellmer. **82**—Colored pencil. **83**—Pencil.

Bellmer

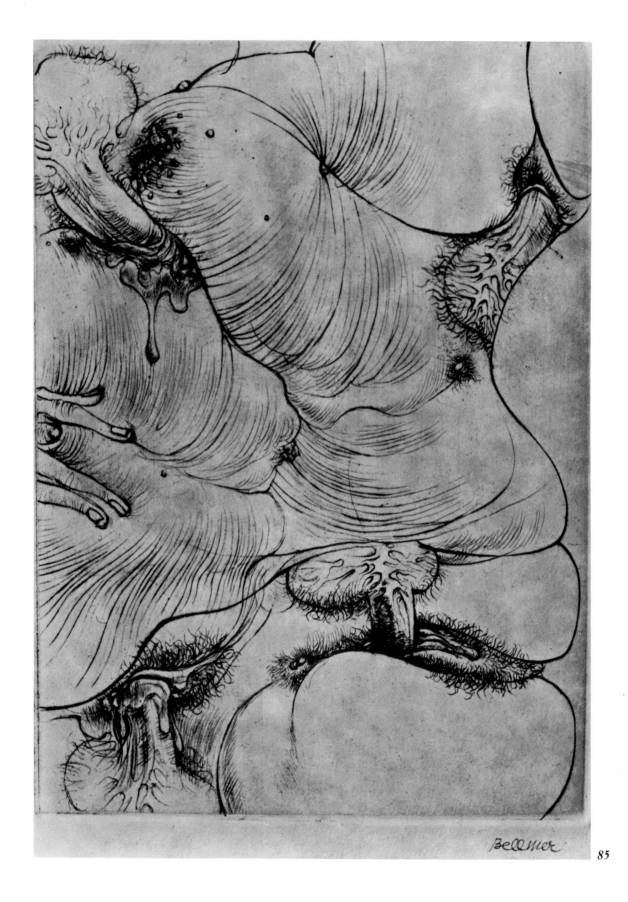

85

Hans Bellmer. 84—Copper engraving. 85—Colored etching.

86

86–87—Pierre Klossowski (France), pencil.

87

88

89

88–90—*Arturo Carmassi (Italy), pencil.*

91

Matta (Chile and France). **91**—*Pencil and colored crayon.* **92–93**—*Etchings.*

92

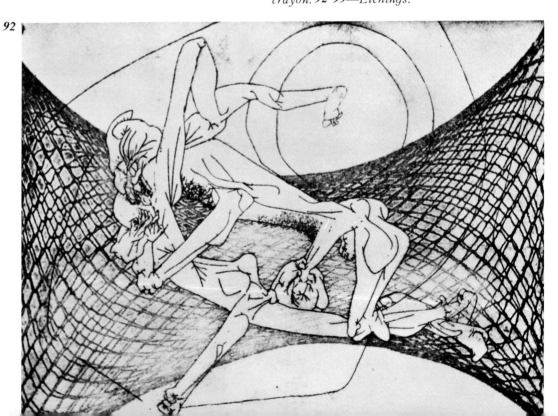

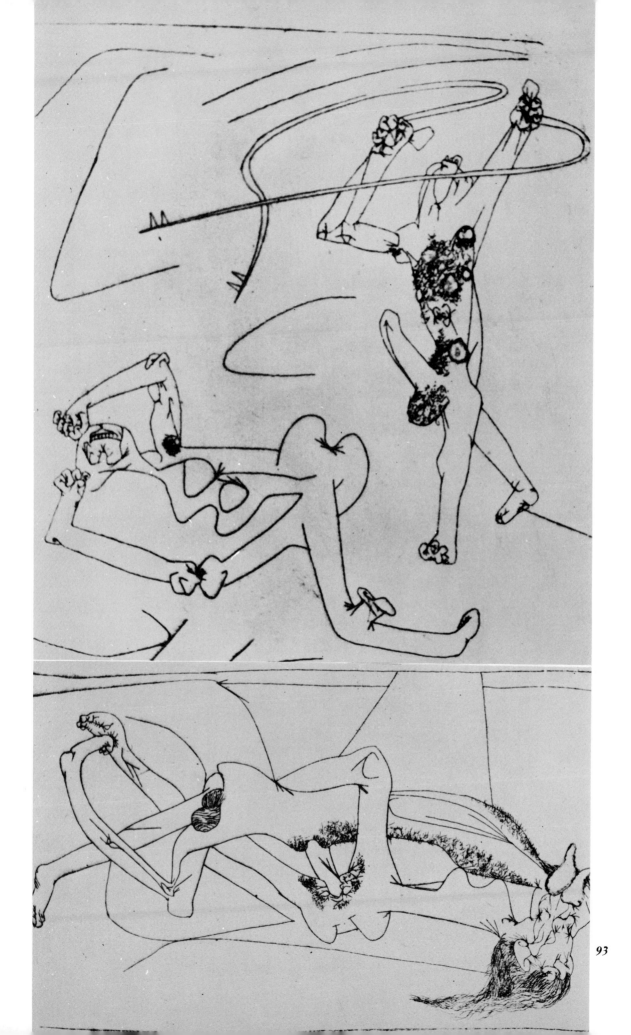

94

95

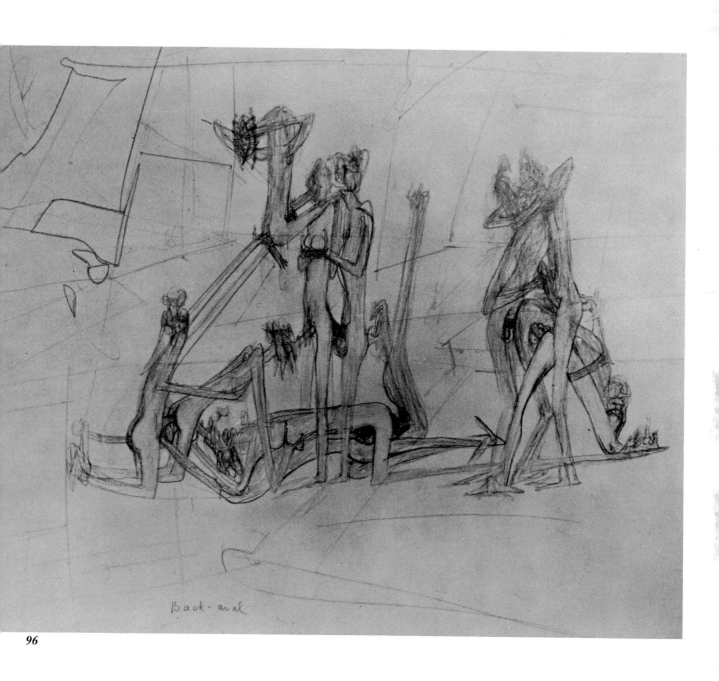

Back-aral

96

94-96—*Matta, pencil and colored crayon.*

97

97—*Melle (Holland), Chinese ink.* **98**—*Yves Tanguy (France and Switzerland), ink.* **99**—*Barbara Nessim (U.S.), "Woman Wearing Headdress," watercolor.*

98

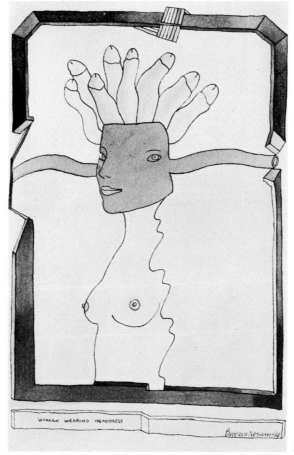

WOMAN WEARING HEADDRESS

Barbara Nessim 46

99

100

101

100-101—Karel Appel (Holland), Chinese ink.

102

103

104

105

Jan Lebenstein (Poland and France). **102–104**—Ink.
105—Oil.

106

107

108

108—Brigid Polk (U.S.), "Hungarian Packing House,"
from Brigid Polk's Cock Book, collage. 109–110—
Andrea Picini (Italy), oil on wood with photomontage.

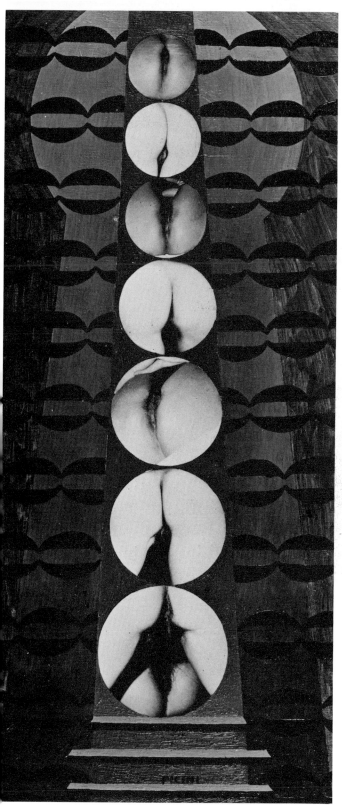

109

110

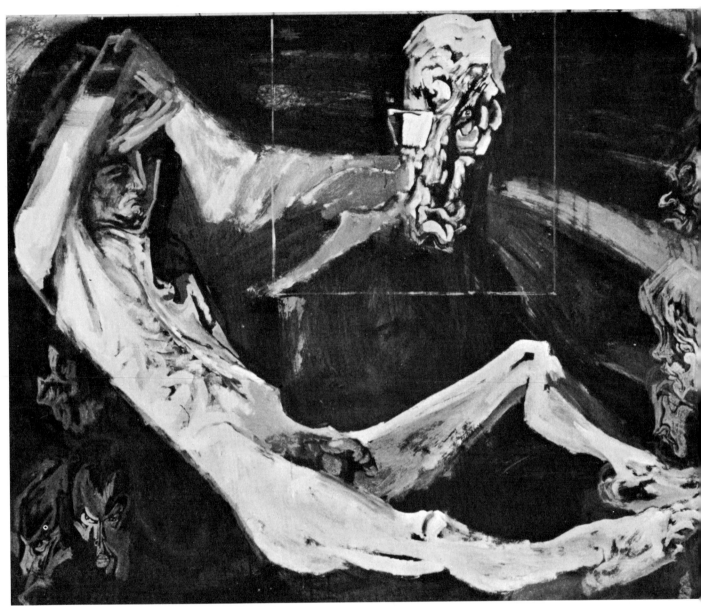

111

111—*Feliks Topolski (Poland and England)*, "*William Burroughs as the author of* Naked Lunch," *oil.*
112—*Anne Marie Brange (Denmark), watercolor.*

n'aura il y aura une fin... commence d'abord par regarder   Anne Marie Brauer 1968.

113

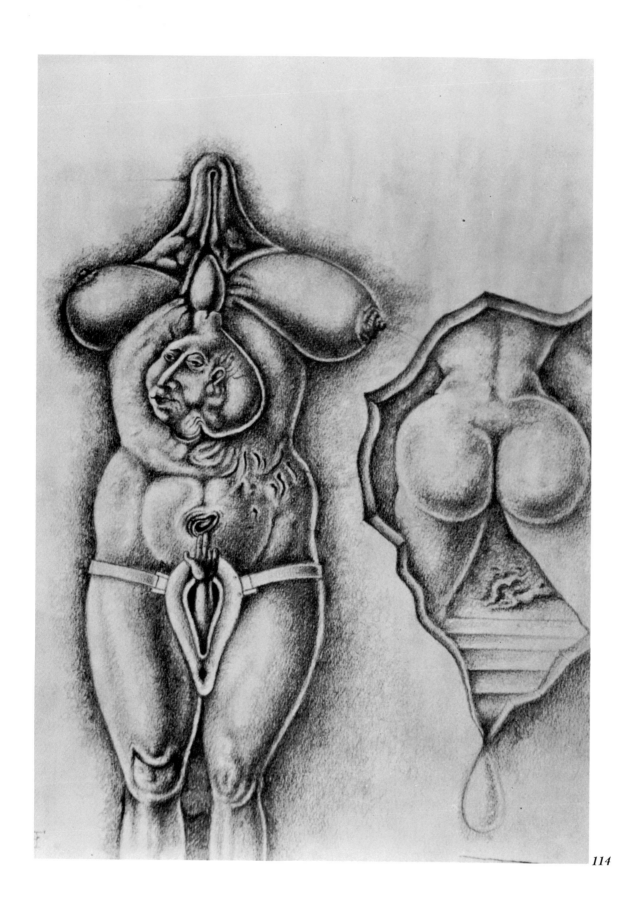

114

113–114—Frédéric Pardo (France), pencil.

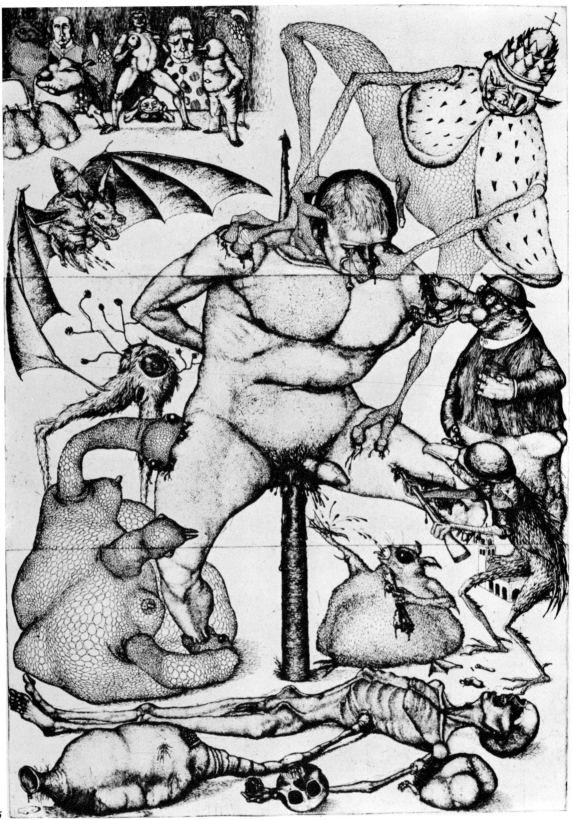

115

116

115—*Carsten Svennson (Denmark), etching.* 116—*Elsje
(Holland), ink.*

117

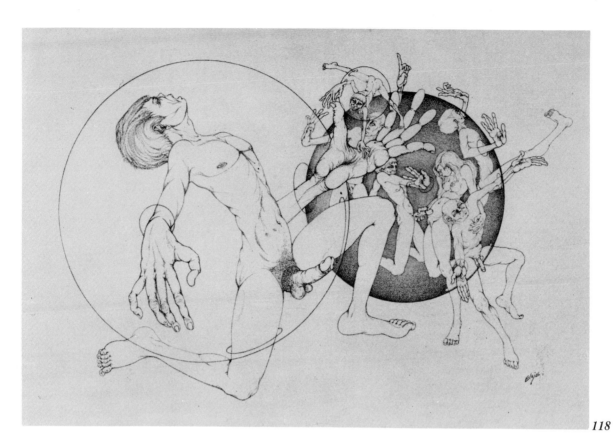

118

119

Elsje. **117**—*Pencil.* **118–119**—*Ink.*

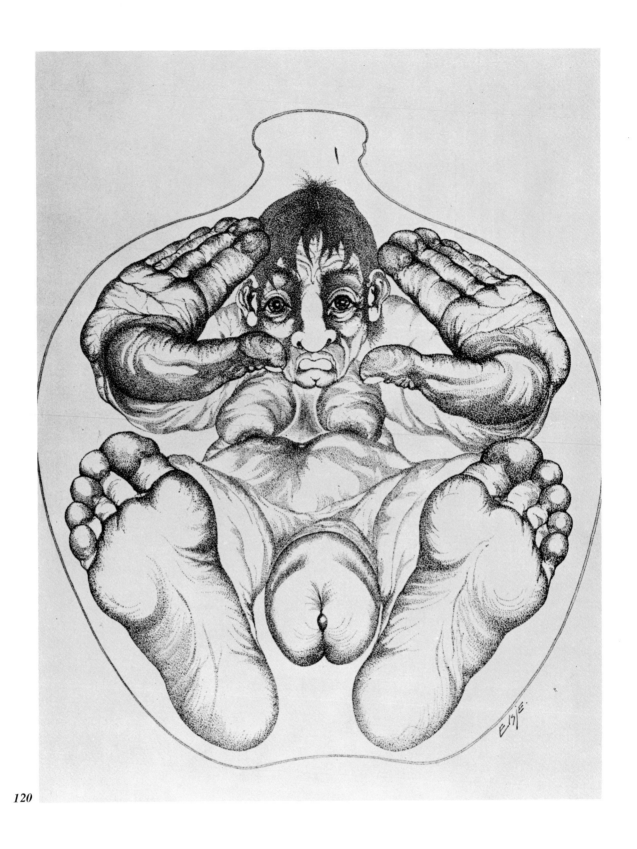

120

Elsje. **120–121**—*Ink.* **122**—*Pastel.*

121

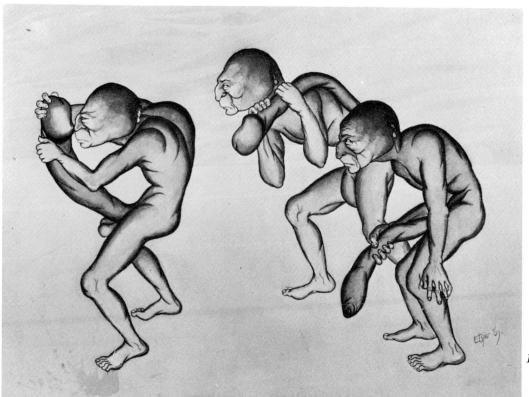

122

123

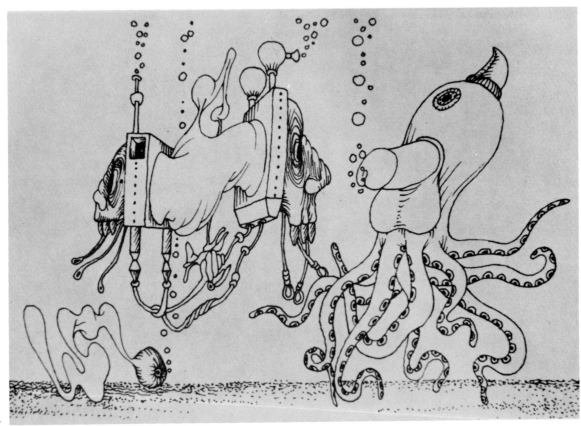

124

Cosmogonie

Alejandro

125

123-125—Ramon Alejandro (Cuba and France), ink.

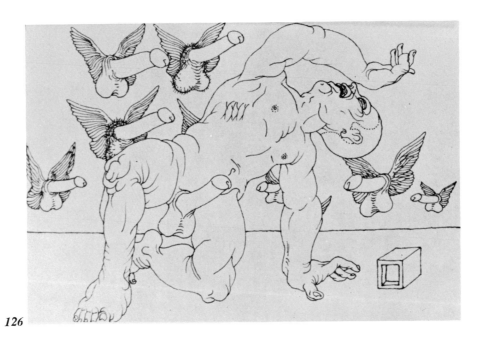

126

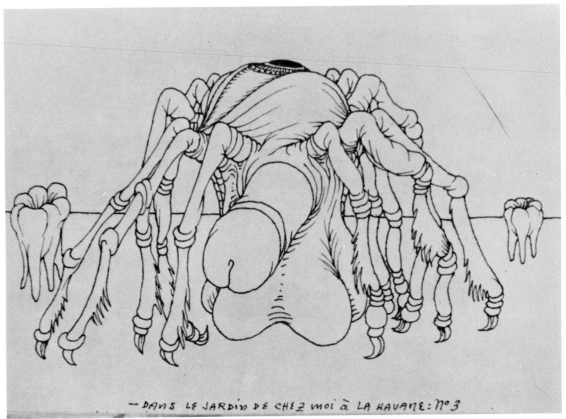

— DANS LE JARDIN DE CHEZ MOI à LA HAVANE: N°3

127

126–130—Ramon Alejandro, ink.

CAFÉ CRÈME:

128   129

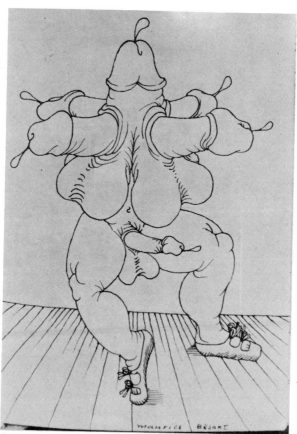

130

97

131

Francis Souza (India and England).
131 and **133**—*Pencil.* **132**—*Ink.*

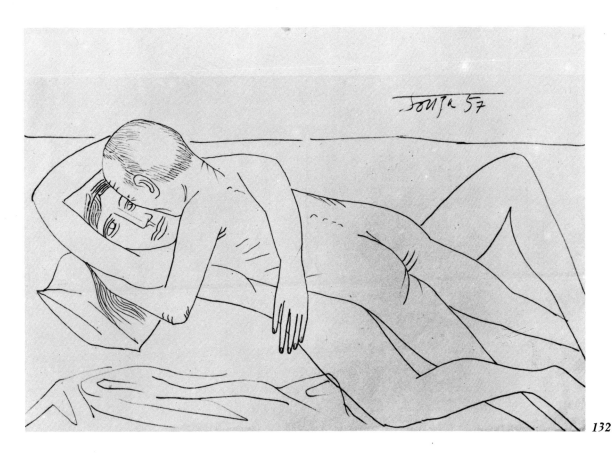

132

133

134

135

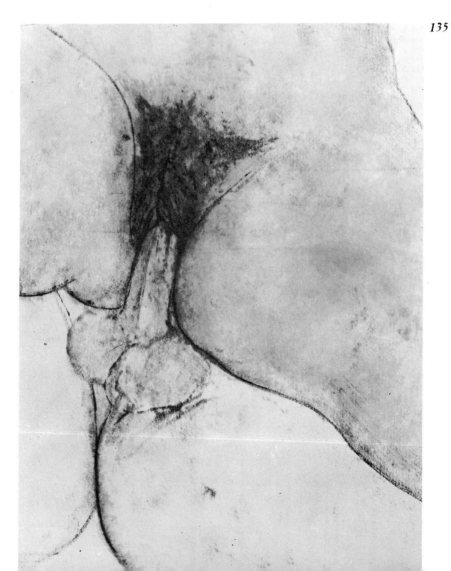

100

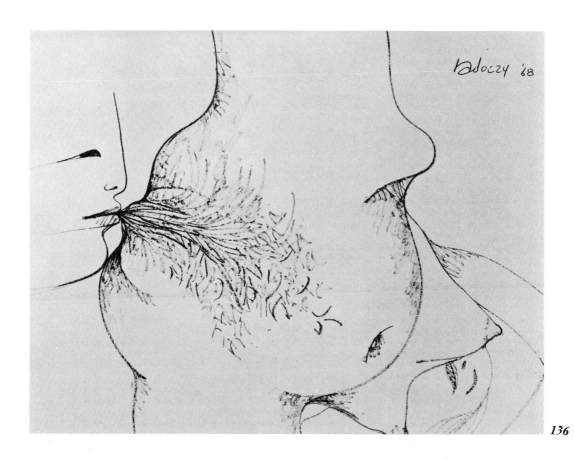

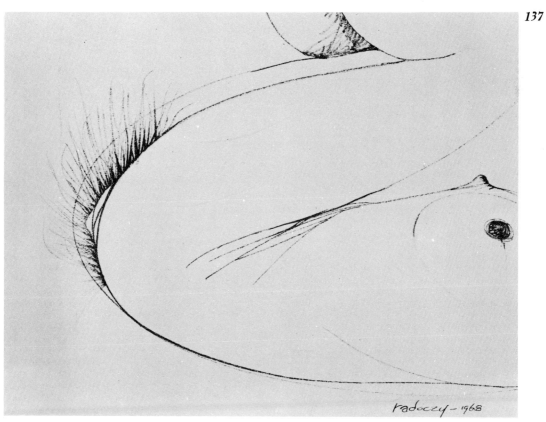

Charles Stark (U.S.). **134**—*Oil monotype.* **135**—*Oil wash and pastel.*
136-137—*Albert Radoczy (U.S.), pencil.*

138

138—Albert Radoczy, "Nude, Red and Yellow," oil.
139—Boris Vansier (France), "La Position," from
the series "Les Offrandes," collage imprégné.
140—Tom Rose (U.S.), colored etching.

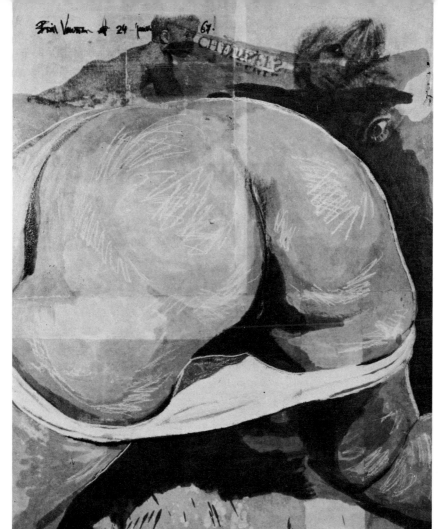

139

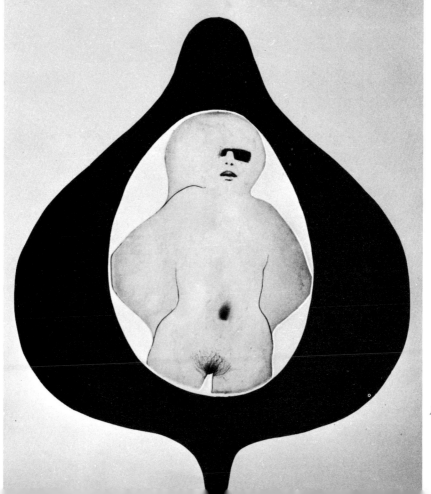

140

141

142

143

144

141-144—Else Maj Johansson (Sweden), lithographs.

cieciovka

flower child

145

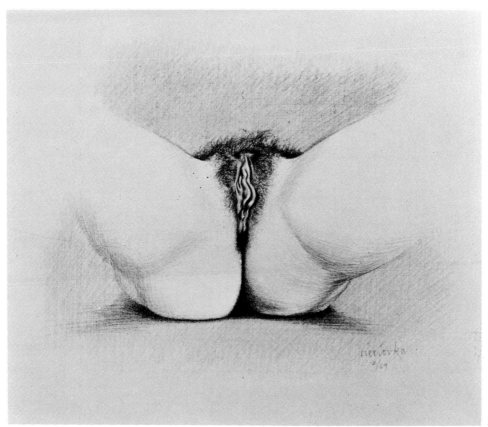

146

147

145–147—Frank Cierciorka (U.S.), pencil.

148

149

150

151

152

A. Raymond Katz (U.S.). **148** and **150–152**—White ink.
149—Ink.

153

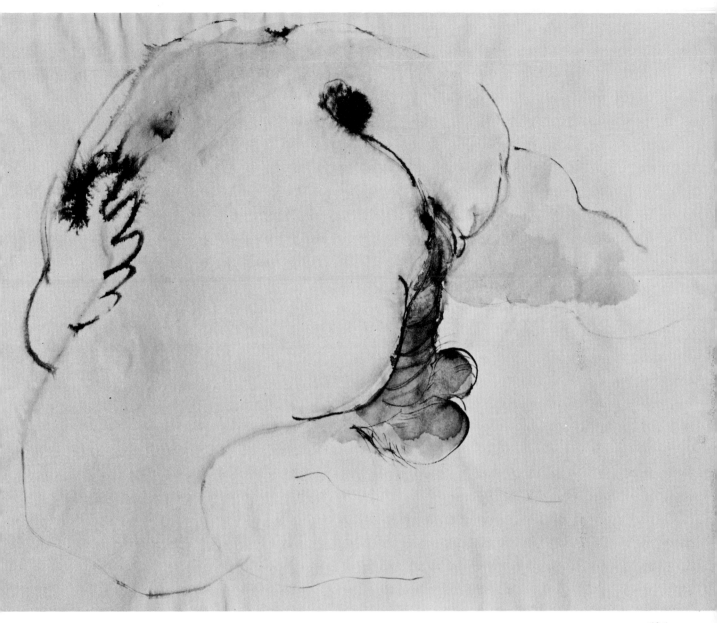

154

153–154—Anne Grete (Sweden), colored ink.

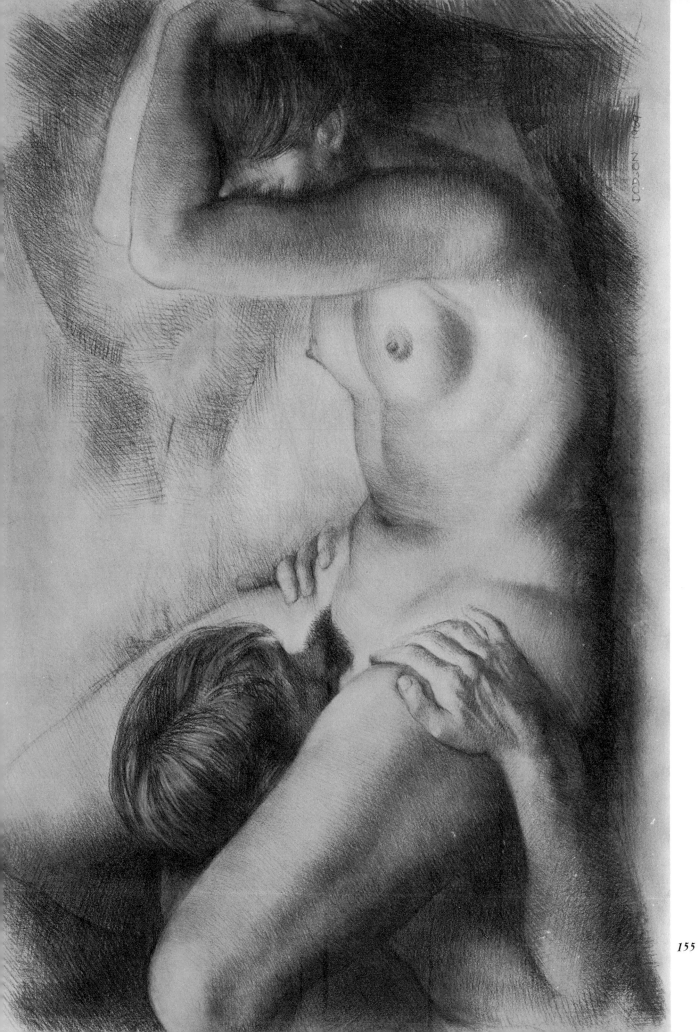

156

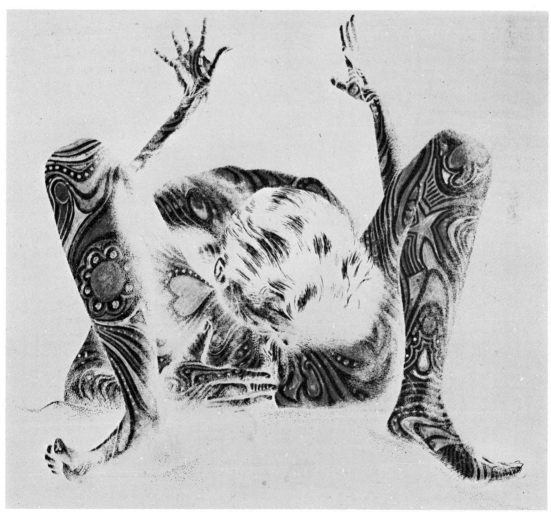

157

*155—Betty Dodson (U.S.), pencil. 156—Borge Sornum
(Denmark), oil on plywood. 157—John Andrews
(U.S.), drawing with color painted on acetate overlay.*

113

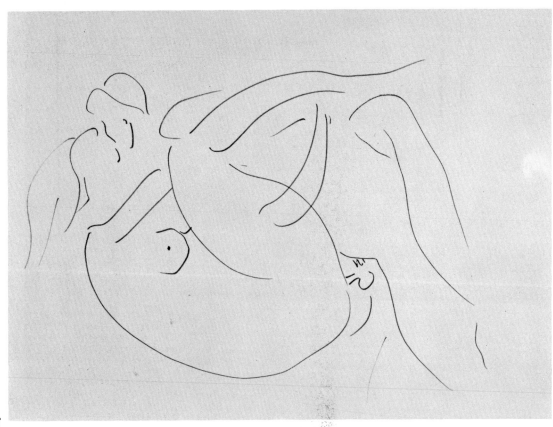

158

159

IX

IX-XII—*Karel Appel (Holland), oil on paper.*

X

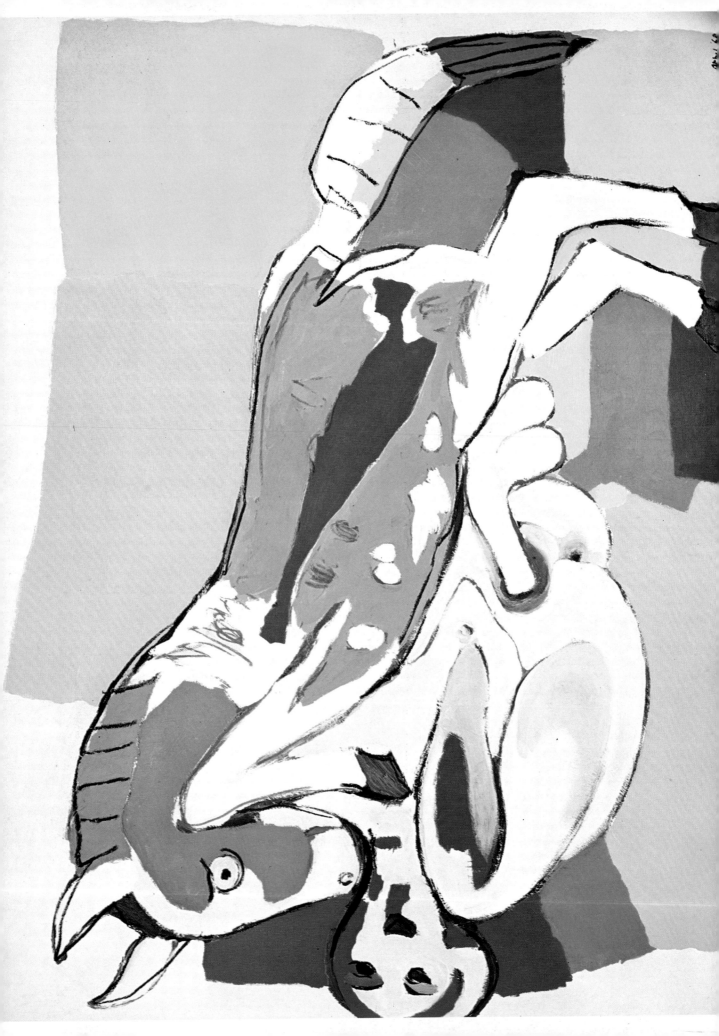

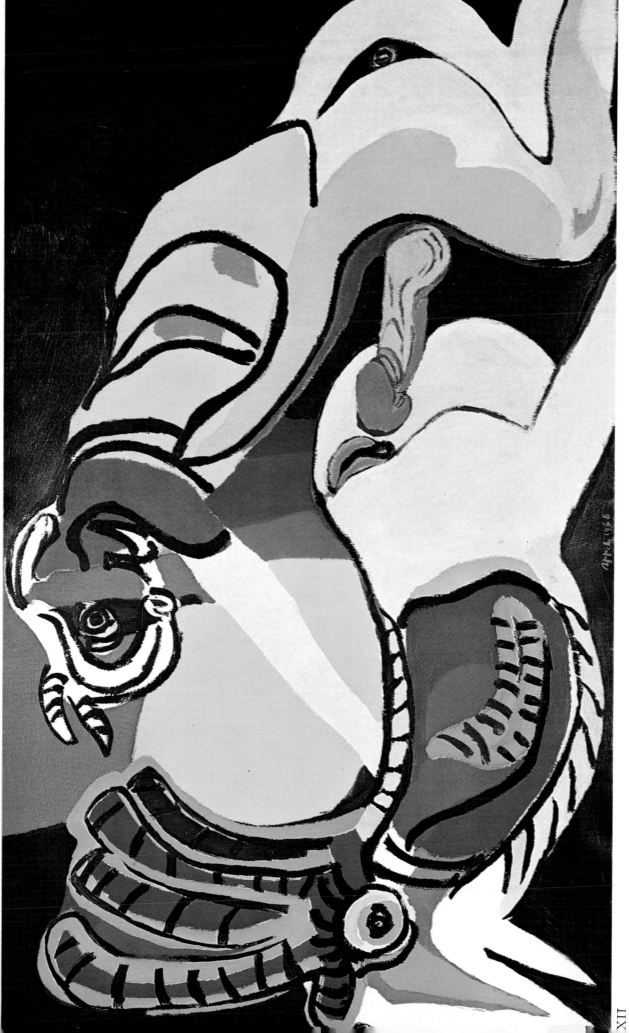

XIII

XIII and XIV— *Karel Appel (Holland), oil on paper*
XV—*M. Pouget (France), crayon and watercolor.*

XIV

XV

XVI

XVI—*Cesare Peverelli (Italy and France), watercolor.*
XVII—*Boris Vansier (Switzerland, of Russian origin),
from the series "Les Offrandes," collage imprégné.*

XVII

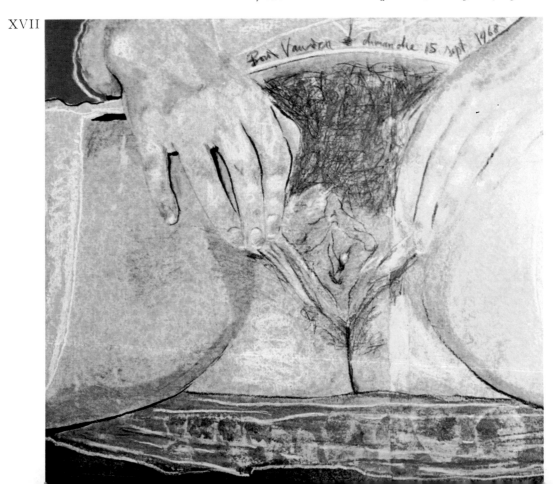

XVIII—*Walasse Ting (China and U.S.), crayon on paper.*

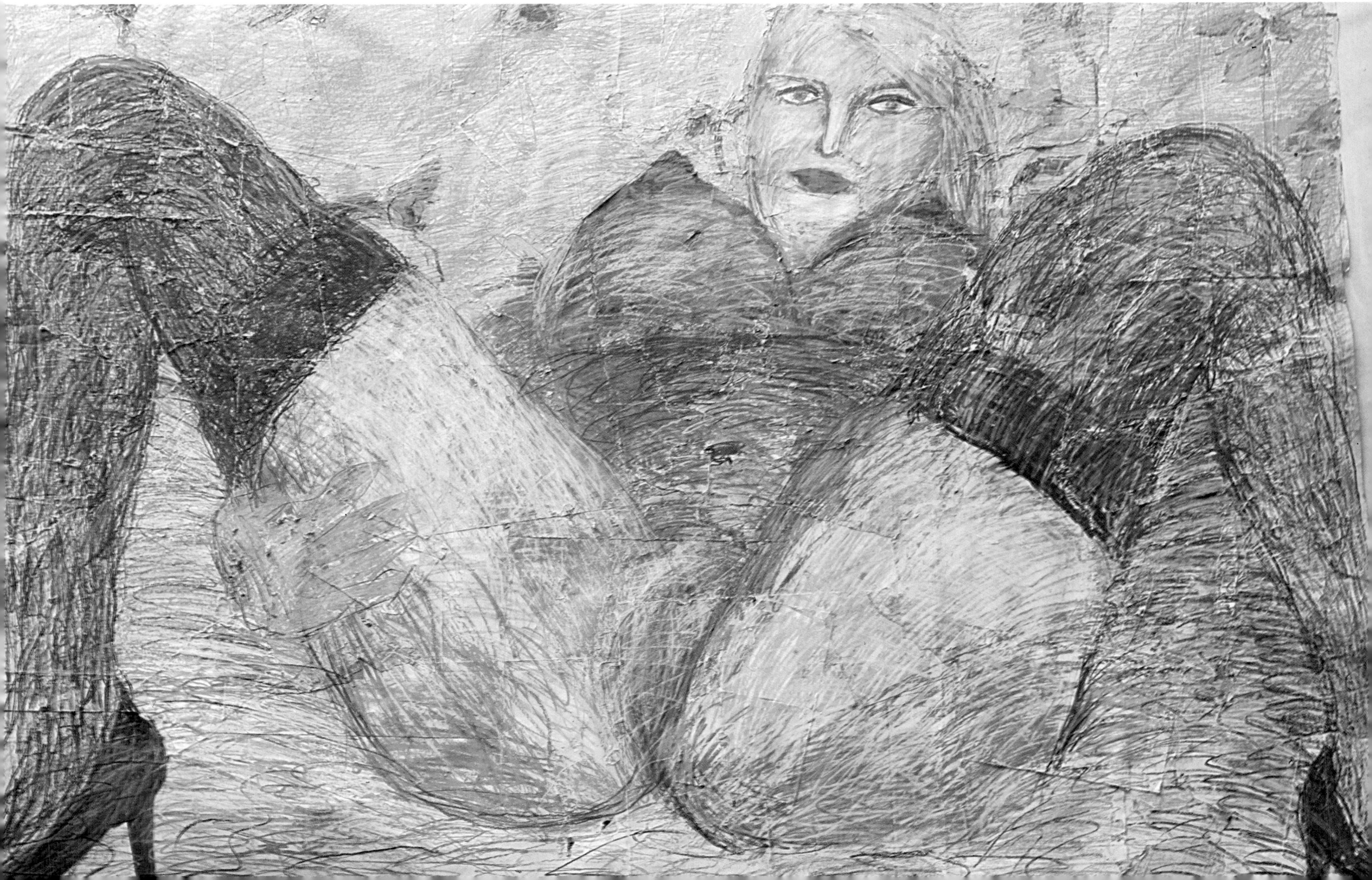

XI

XX

XIX and XX—*Max Walter Svanberg (Sweden), collage.*

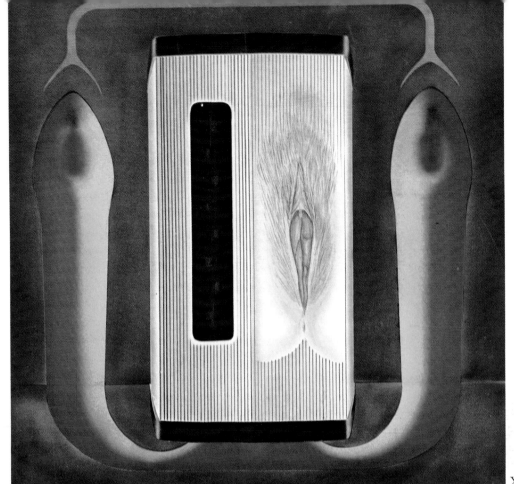

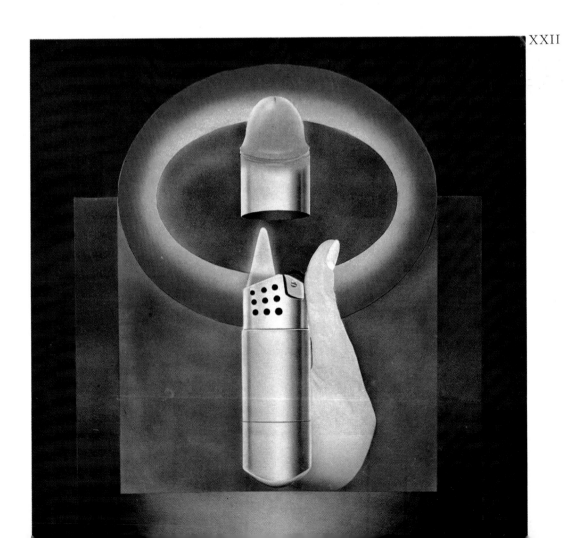

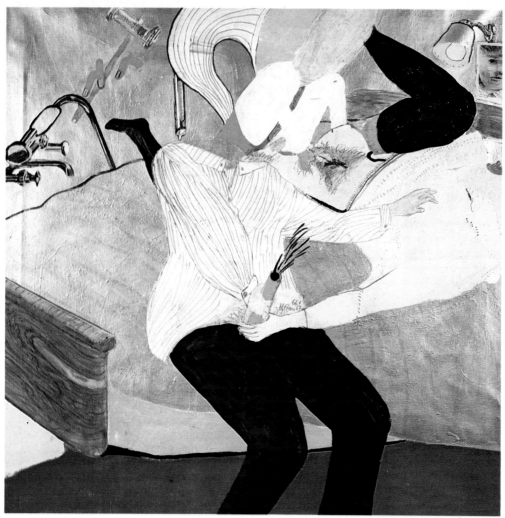

XXIII

XXI and XXII—*Alfred Beloch (Germany), painting on cardboard with colors used for correction of printer's plates.*
XXIII—*Heimrad Prem (Germany), oil on canvas.*

XXV

XXIV—*Amarol (U.S.), colored-ink.*
XXV—*Kerstin Apelman Öberg (Sweden), "Noah's Ark," watercolor.*
XXVI—*Stella Svedberg (10-year-old Swedish girl), watercolor.*

XXVI

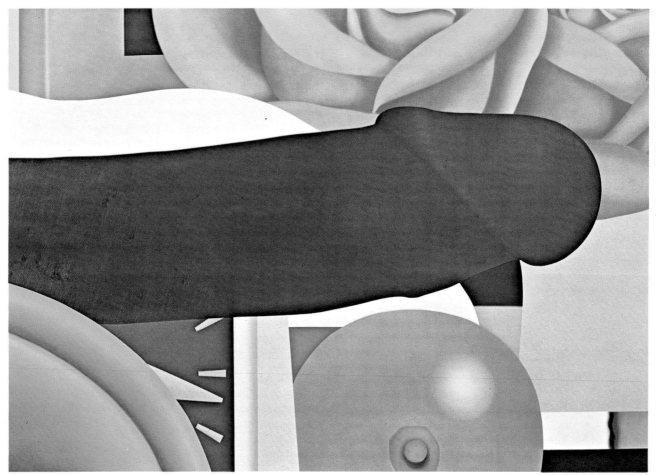

XXVII

XXVII—*Tom Wesselmann (U.S.), "Bedroom Painting #20," 1969, oil; courtesy Sidney Janis Gallery.*

XXVIII

XXVIII—*Mel Ramos (U.S.), "Walrus," 1967, oil.*

XXIX

XXIX—*John Andrews (U.S.), drawing with color painted on acetate overlay.*

XXX

XXX—*Bob Stanley (U.S.), silkscreen from On 1st deck of playing cards.*

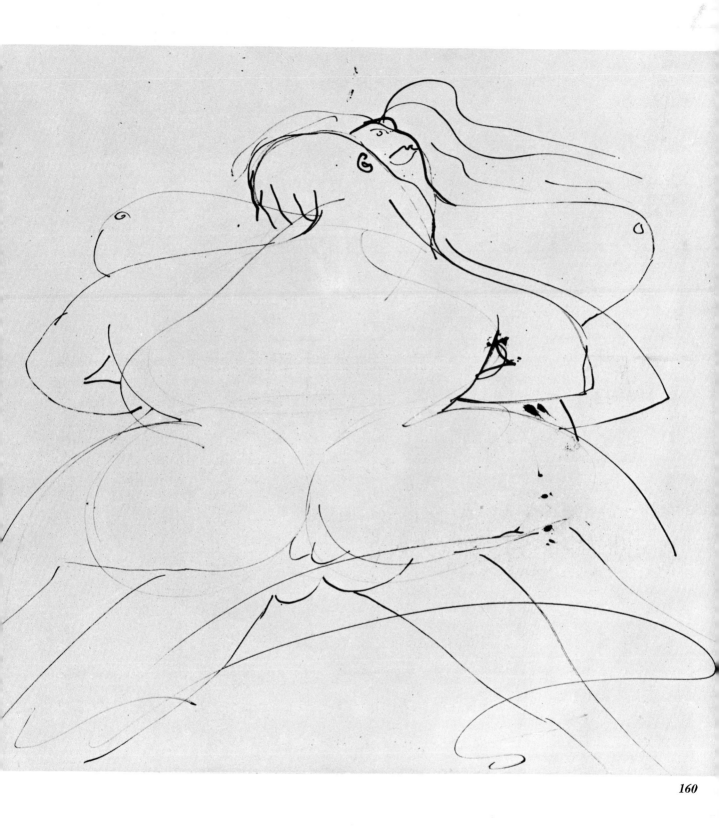

160

158–159—*Robert Jon (China and U.S.), ink.* **160**—*Sam Francis (U.S.), "Blue Stick Pink," black ink (collection Walasse Ting).*

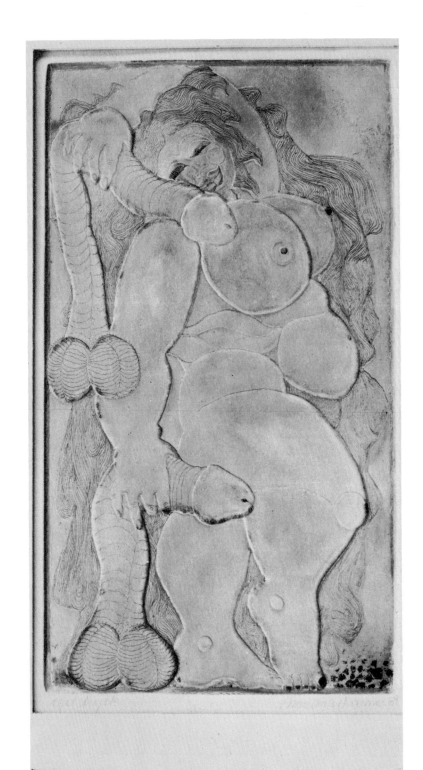

Jag är ett ringa blomster i Saron, en lilja i dalen.
Vederkvicken mig med drufvakor, styrken mig
med äpplen; ty jag är sjuk av kärlek.

161

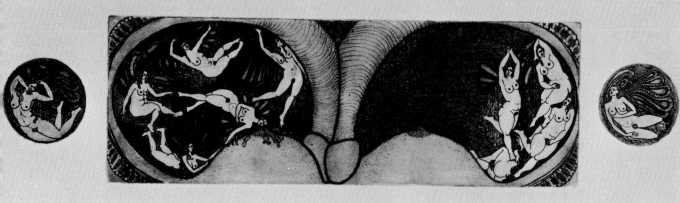

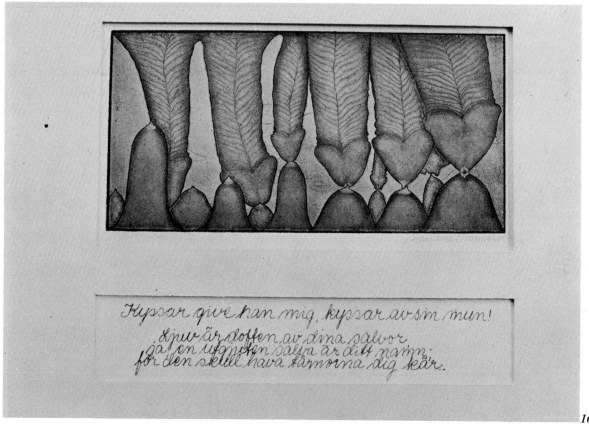

Kyssar give han mig, kyssar av sin mun!
ljuv är doften av dina salvor,
ja, en utgjuten salva är ditt namn;
för den skull hava tärnorna dig kär.

161–163—*Mariana Manner (Sweden), colored etchings.*

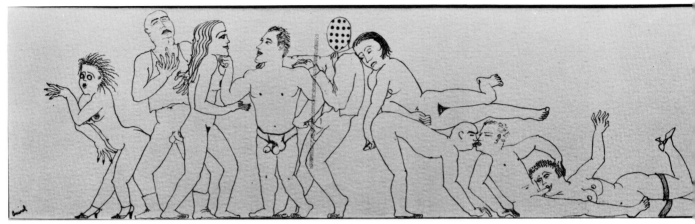

164

165

*Amarol (U.S.). **164** and **167**—Ink. **165–166**—Colored ink.*

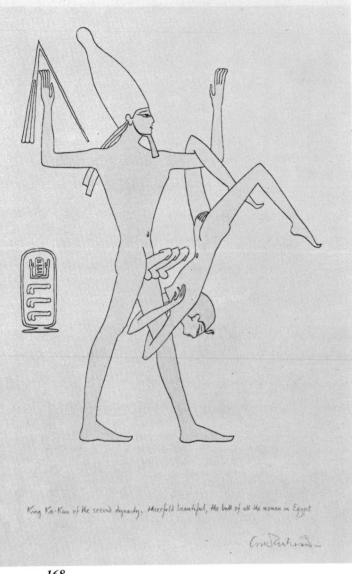

King Ka-Kau of the second dynasty, threefold beautiful, the bull of all the women in Egypt

168

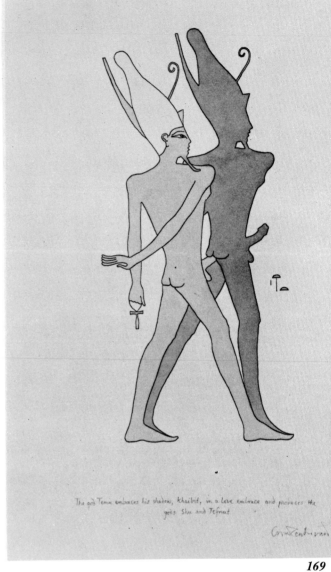

The god Temu embraces his shadow, khaibit, in a love embrace and produces the gods Shu and Tefnut.

169

Oscar Reutersvärd (Sweden), watercolors. **168**—"The god Temu embraces his shadow, Khaibit, in a love embrace and produces the gods Shū and Tefnut." **169**—"King Ka-Kau of the second dynasty, threefold beautiful, the bull of all the women in Egypt." **170**—Rē-Atum, the All, Lord of Assiūt, has union with the divine Hand and procreates the first pair, Shū and Tefnut."
171—"Alexander the Great before the God Nim at Karnak."

Rē-Atum, the All, lord of Aesūē, has union with the divine Hand and procreates the first pair, Shu and Tefnut

170

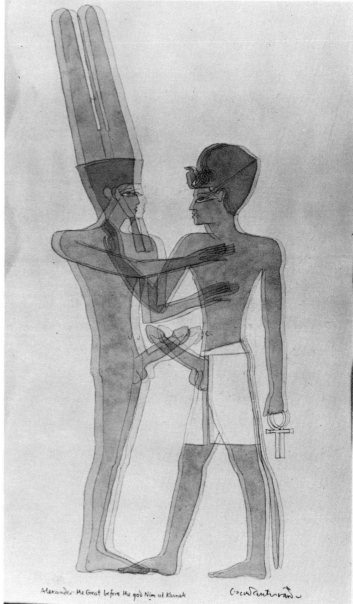

Alexander the Great before the god Nin at Karnak

171

172

173

122

174

172–173—*Dorothy Iannone (U.S.), "Dialogues,"*
watercolor. **174**—*Sven Dalsgård (Denmark),*
watercolor.

123

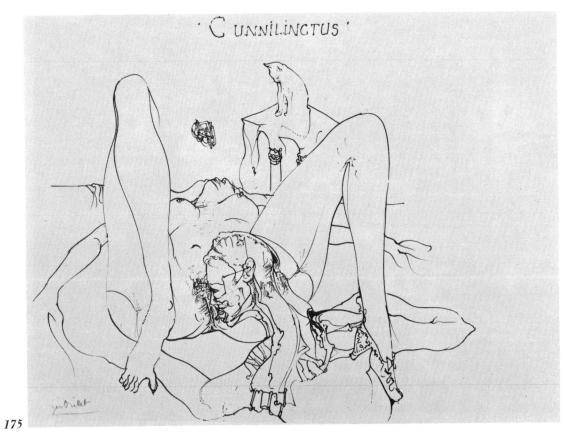

'CUNNILINCTUS'

175

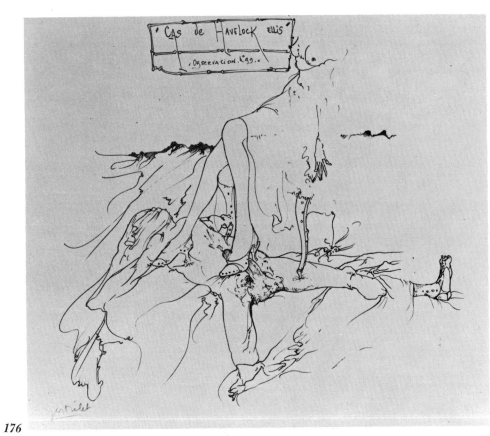

'CAS de HAVELOCK ELLIS'

·OBSERVATION.L.99.·

176

124

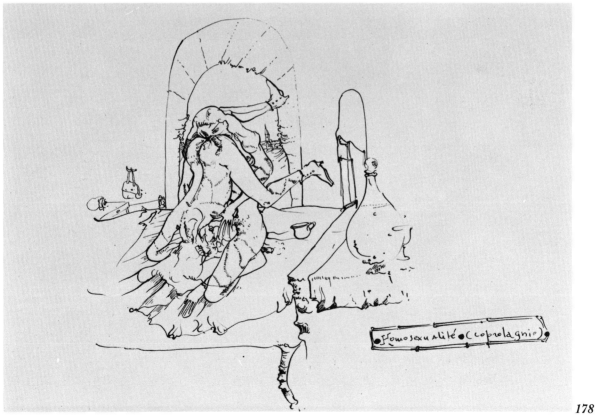

175–178—*Yves Milet (France), illustrations to Krafft-Ebing's* Psychopathia Sexualis, *ink.*

179

180

181

182

179–182—*Mario Tauzin (France), offset prints from copperplates.*

183

184

185

186

183–186—*Mario Tauzin, offset prints from copperplates.*

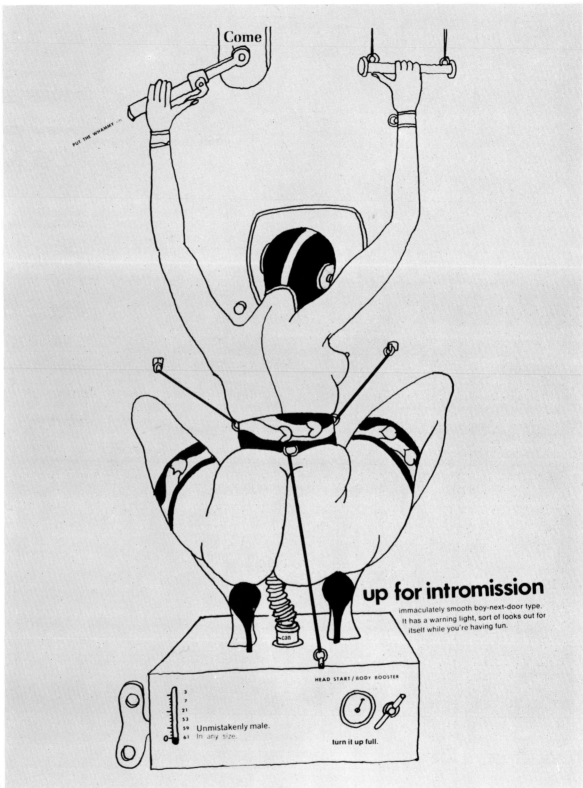

up for intromission

188

Tomi Ungerer (U.S. and France). **187**—*Lithograph.*
188—*Colored ink.*

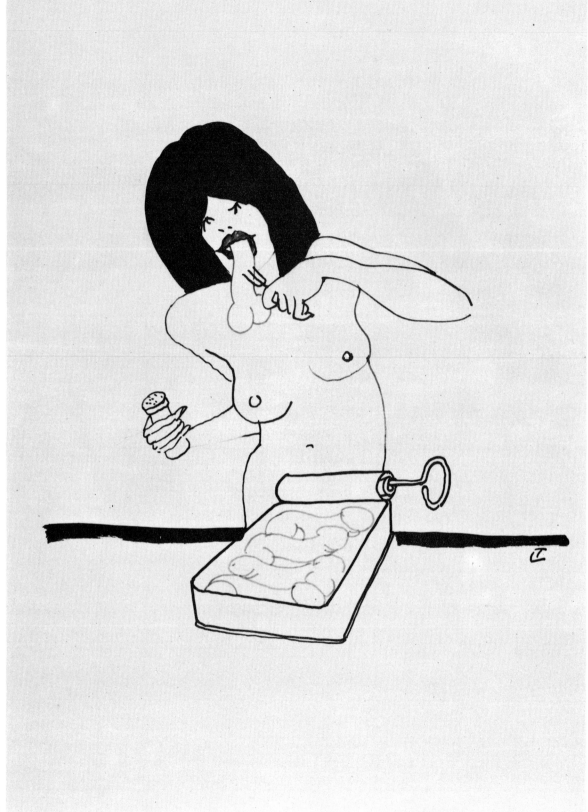

189

189–190—*Tomi Ungerer, colored ink.*

191

192

193

191–193—Ulf Rahmberg (Sweden), watercolors.

194

Ulf Rahmberg. **194** *and* **196**—*Watercolors.* **195**—*Collage and pencil.*

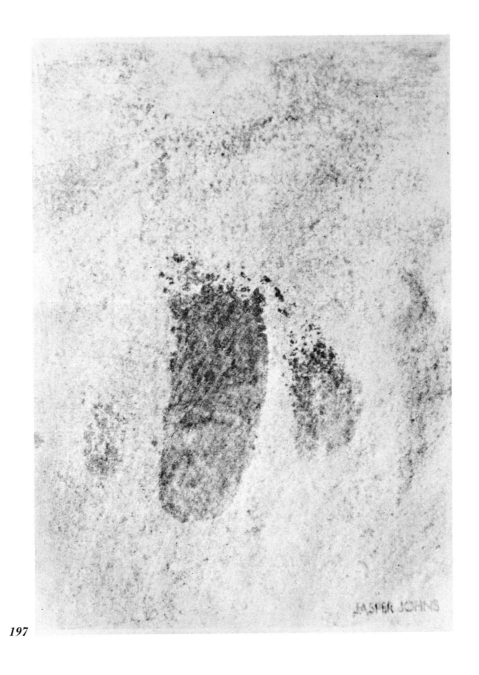

197

197—Jasper Johns (U.S.), charcoal on paper (from Brigid Polk's Cock Book).

198 199

Larry Rivers (U.S.) **198**—"Frank, Nude," oil.
199—"America's No. 1 Problem," mixed media.

200 Caprice Mon   CO 66

201   CO 65

202

203

200—*Claes Oldenburg (Sweden and U.S.), "Capric Monument," 1967, crayon, casein (collection John and Kimiko Powers; photo courtesy Sidney Janis Gallery).*
201—*Claes Oldenburg, "Woman With A Giant Penis Leaning On A Station Wagon," ink.*
Tom Wesselman (U.S.). *202*—*Pencil.* *203*—*"Study for Seascape #28," pencil.*

204

205

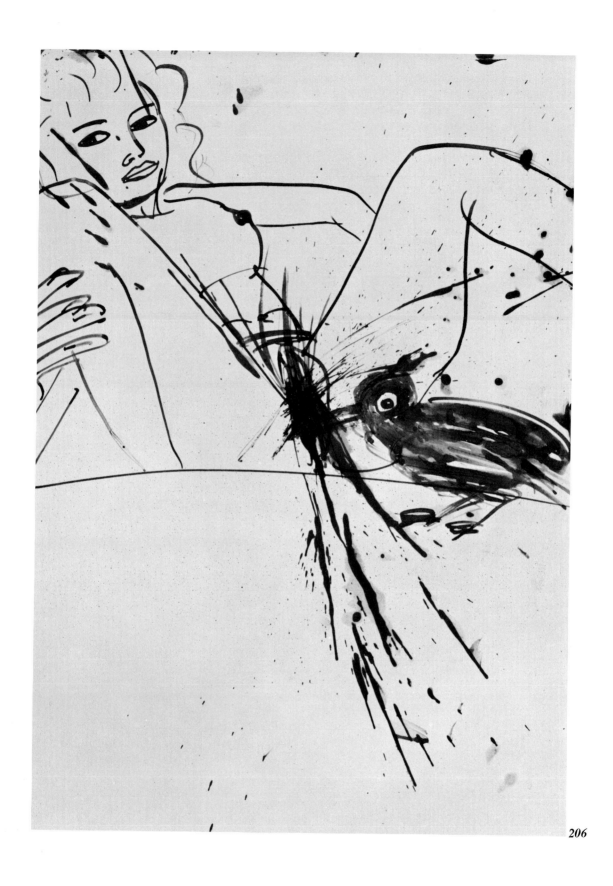

206

Mel Ramos (U.S.). **204**—"Tamanda," pencil, 1968.
205—"Wallaby," pencil, 1967.
206—Walasse Ting (China and U.S.), "Licorice
Flavor," ink.

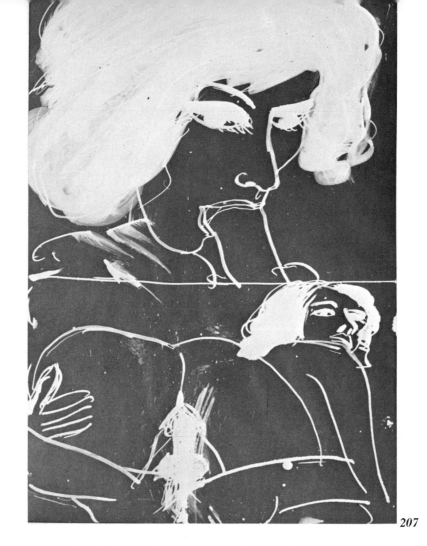

207

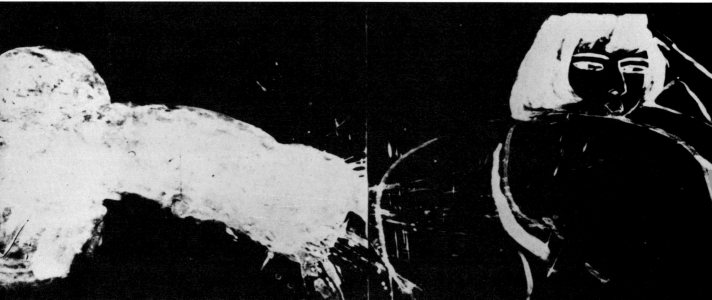

209

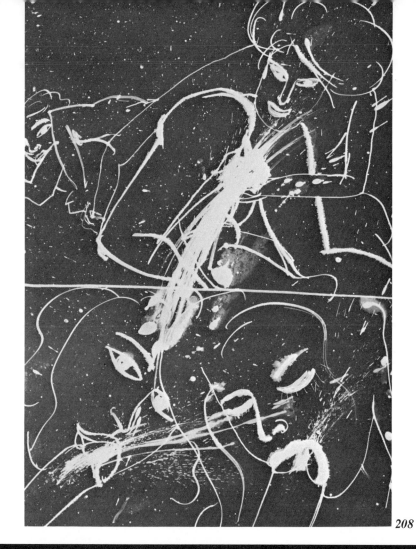

208

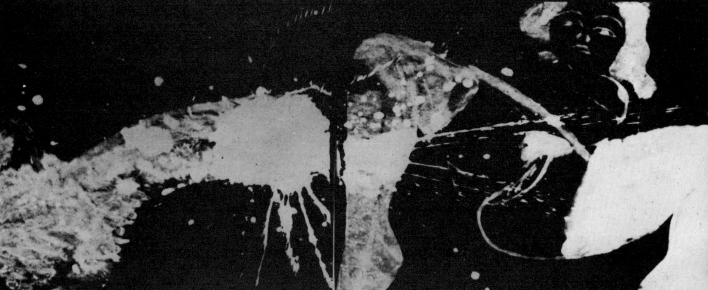

210

Walasse Ting. **207**—"Raspberry Flavor," ink. **208**—
"Chocolate Flavor," ink. **209**—"Chinese Ink," ink.
210—"American Ink," ink.

211

211—*William Copley (U.S.), oil.* **212–213**—*Andy Warhol (U.S.), "Blue Movie," proposals for silkscreen (collection Arnold Leo).*

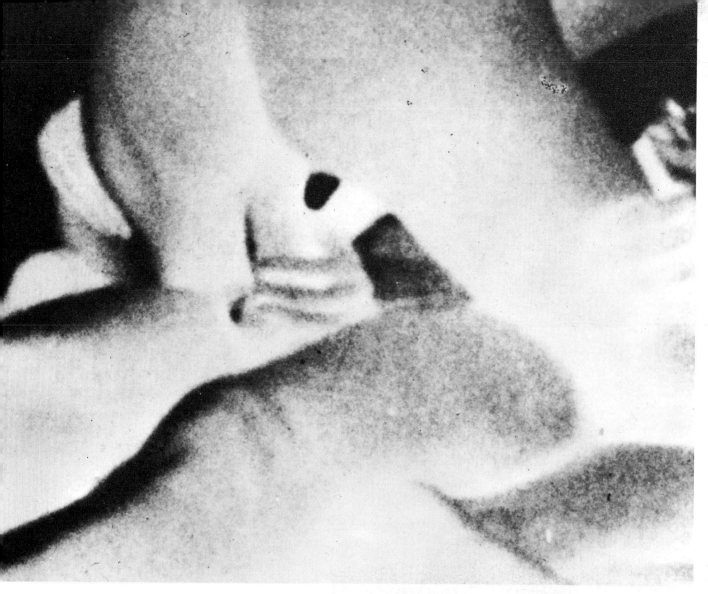

212

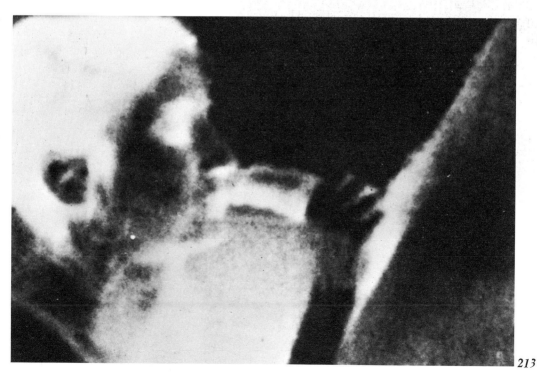

213

214

215

Robert Stanley (U.S.). **214**—"Black and White Head,"
Liquitex on canvas, 1966. **215**—"Red and Black
Pillows," Liquitex on canvas, 1966 (collection John and
Kimiko Powers).

216

216—*Robert Stanley, silkscreen.* 217—*Ulf Rahmberg,
collage and watercolor.*

217

218

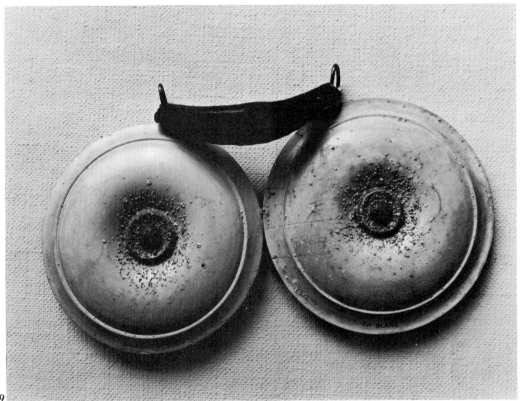

219

220

218—*Anonymous late-17th-century miniature of un-*
known provenance, watercolor on paper. A rare early
example of the once popular trick pictures in which
genitalia or sexual acts are used to form "portraits" that
were sometimes caricatures of real people, but more often
were merely stylized faces. 219—*Pfriem (U.S.), painted*
object. 220—*Hans Bellmer, painted aluminum.*

221

222

154

223

221–222—*Helge Holmskov (Denmark), clay.*
223—*Kaj Nielsen (Denmark), plaster of Paris.*

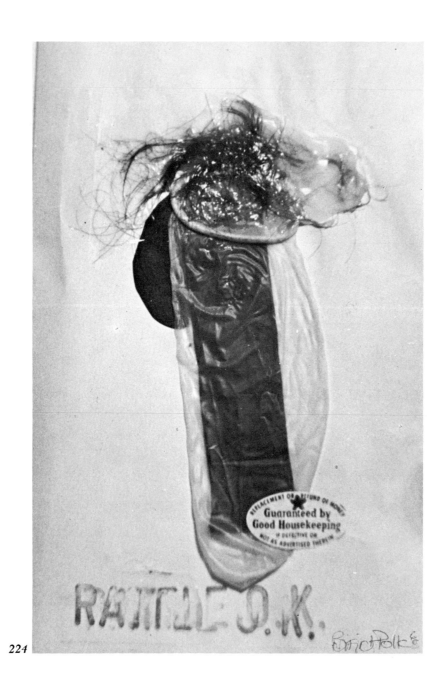

224

224—Brigid Polk (U.S.), "Rattle O.K.," from Brigid Polk's Cock Book, *collage.* ***225***—*Robert Rauschenberg (U.S.), "Carnal Clock I," silkscreen on plexiglass with mirrored surface.* ***226***—*Kiki Kogelnik (U.S.), "Swing in Central Park," proposed public facility.*

225

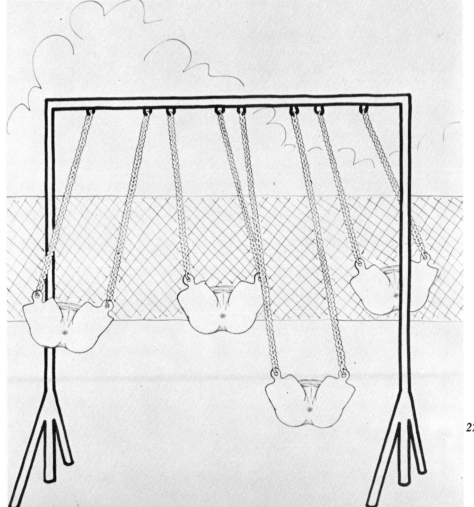

226

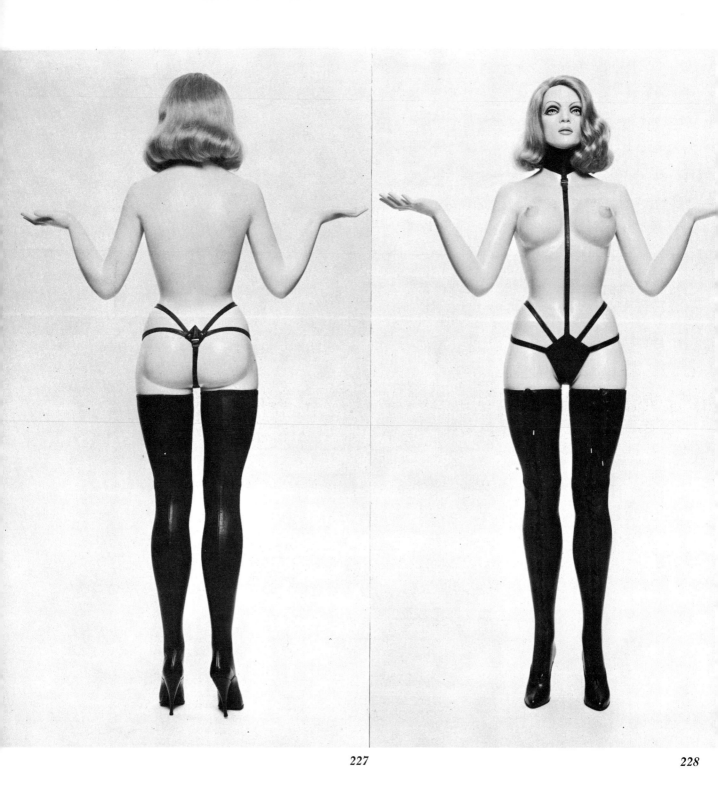

227

228

Allen Jones (England). **227–228**—"Hatstand,"
life-size sculpture, painted glass fiber and resin.
229–230—"Table," *life-size sculpture, painted
glass fiber and resin.*

229

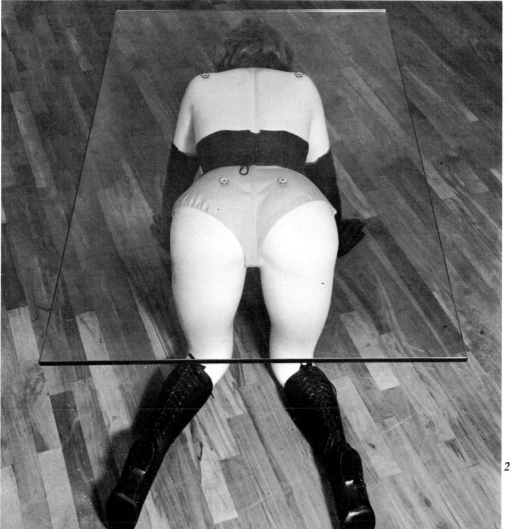

230

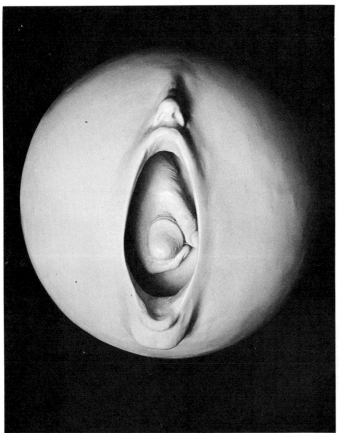

231

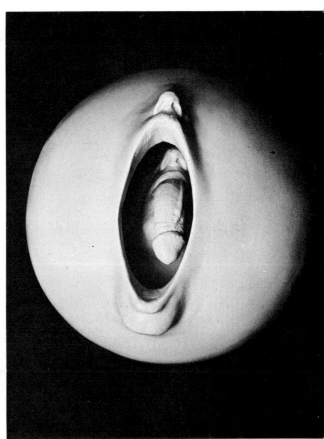

232

233

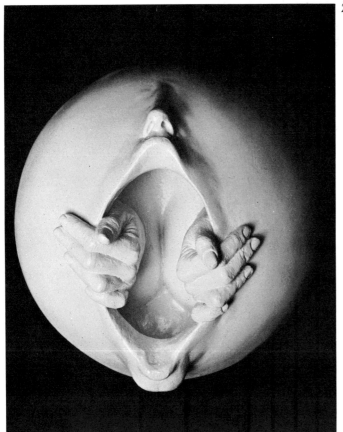

Richard Etts (U.S.). **231**—*"Luna 8," hydrocal.*
232—*"Luna 9," hydrocal.* **233**—*"Luna 6," hydrocal.*
(Photos courtesy Robert Rosinek,
Gallery of Erotic Art.)

234

234—Colima pottery (Pre-Columbian Mexico).

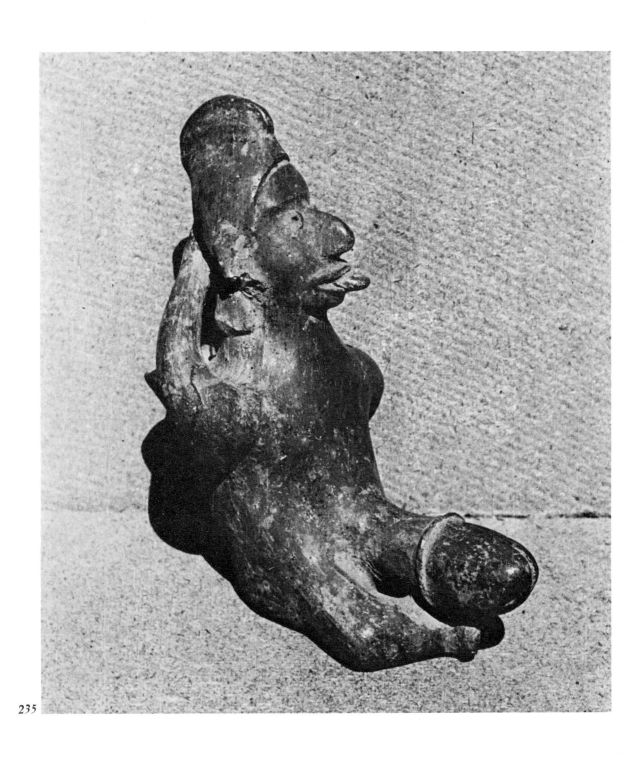

235

235—*Colima pottery (Pre-Columbian Mexico).*
236—*Chimu pottery (Pre-Columbian Peru).*

237

238

237–238—*Chimu pottery (Pre-Columbian Peru).*

239

240

239—*Colima pottery (Pre-Columbian Mexico).*
240—*Chimu pottery (Pre-Columbian Peru).*

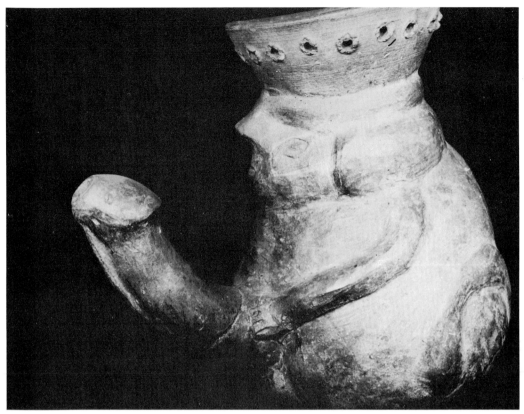

241

242

241–242—Mochica pottery (Pre-Columbian Peru).

243

243—Miniature on ivory, 19th century.

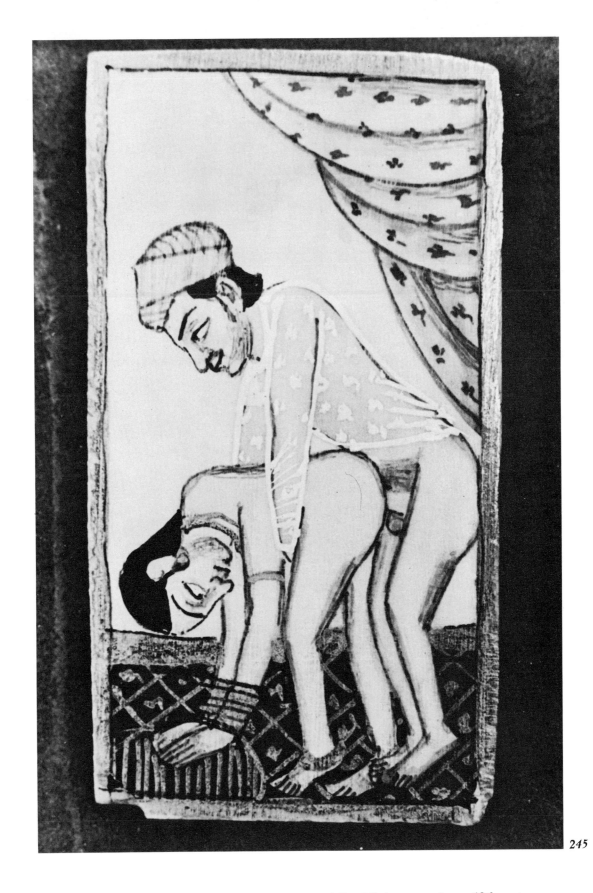

245

244–245—Miniatures on ivory, 19th century.

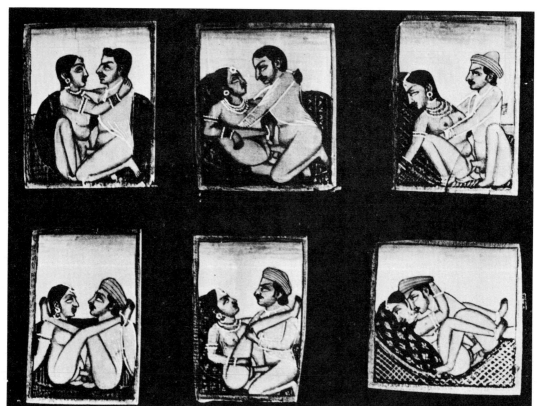

246

246–247—*Miniatures on ivory, 19th century.*

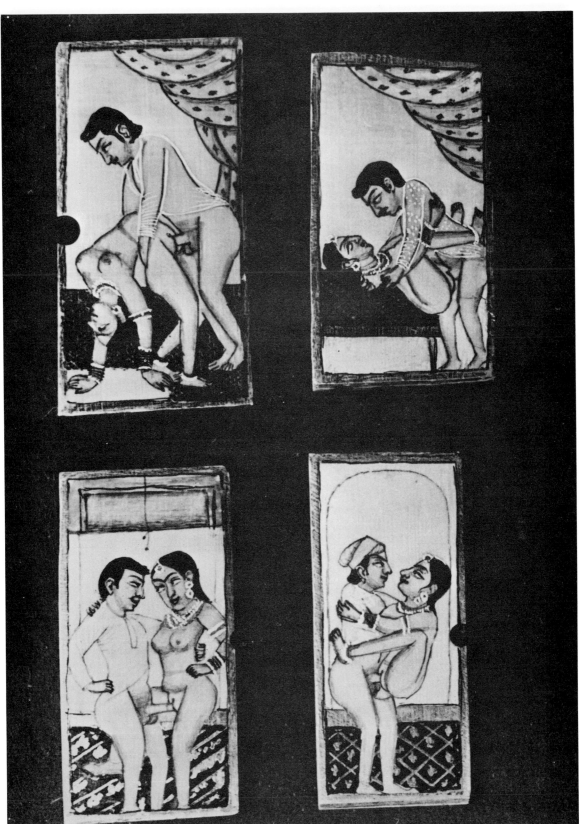

247

248   249

250

248–250—*Miniatures on ivory, 19th century.* **251**—*Fragment of 19th-century watercolor.* **252**—*Primitive painting on paper, ca. 1840.*

251

252

253

254

255

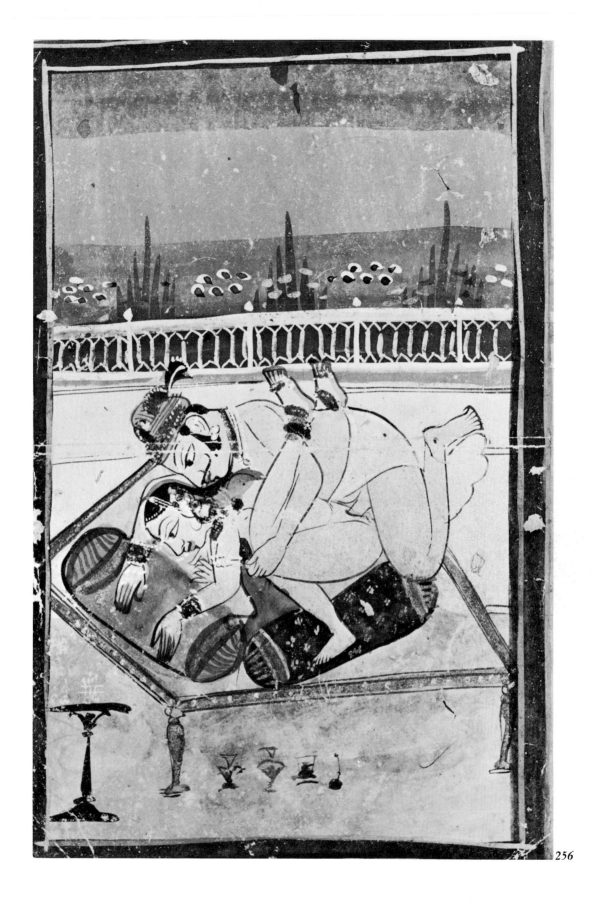

256

255–256—Fine watercolors, ca. 18th century.

257

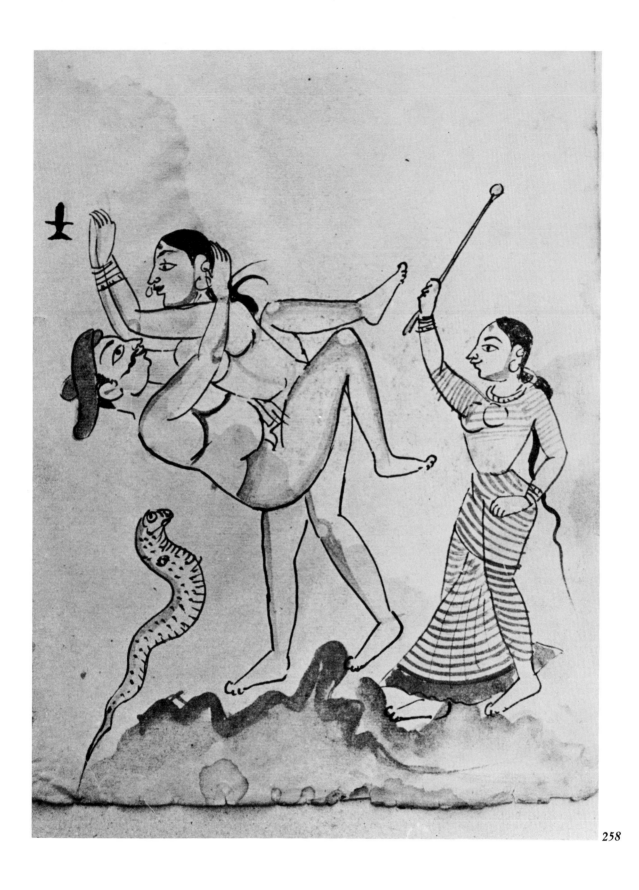

257-258—*Watercolors, Bengal style, ca. 18th century.*

259

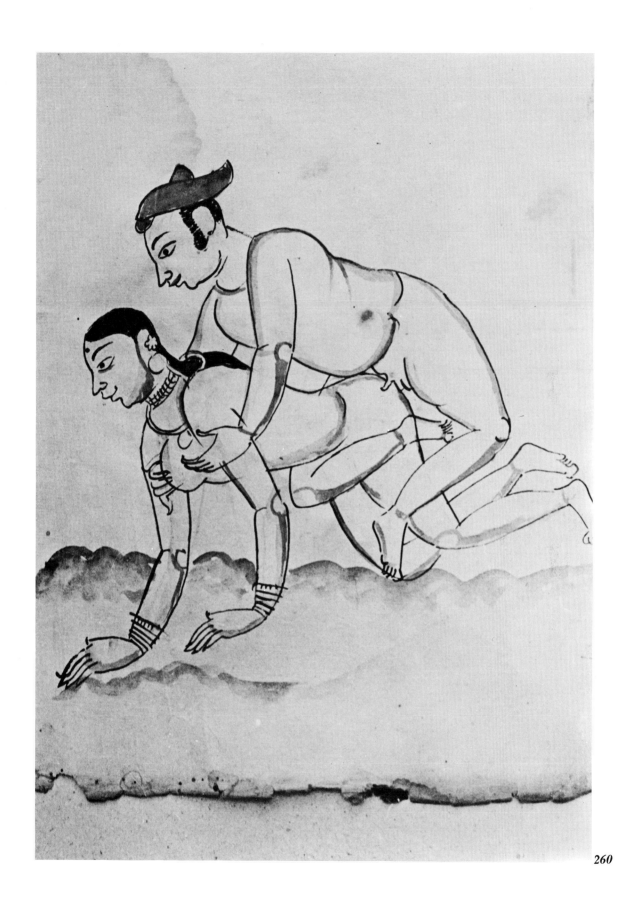

260

259–260—Watercolors, Bengal style, ca. 18th century.

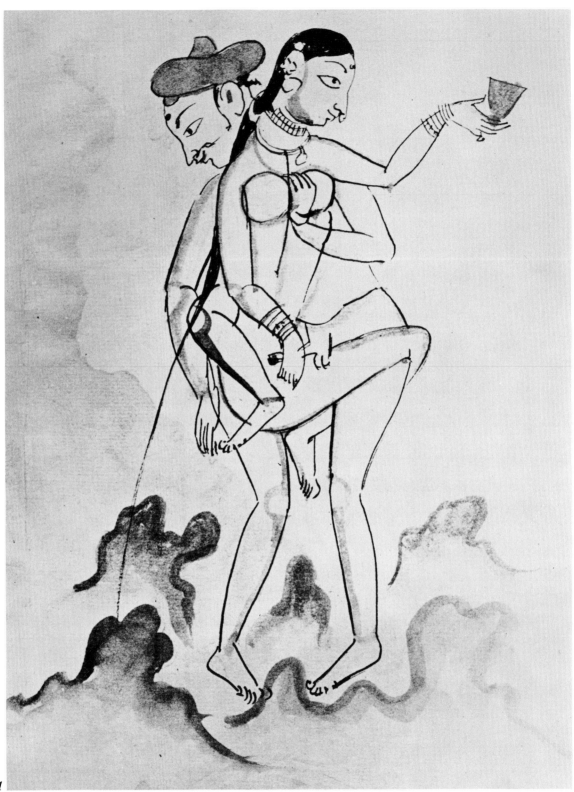

261

261-262—*Watercolors, Bengal style, ca. 18th century.*

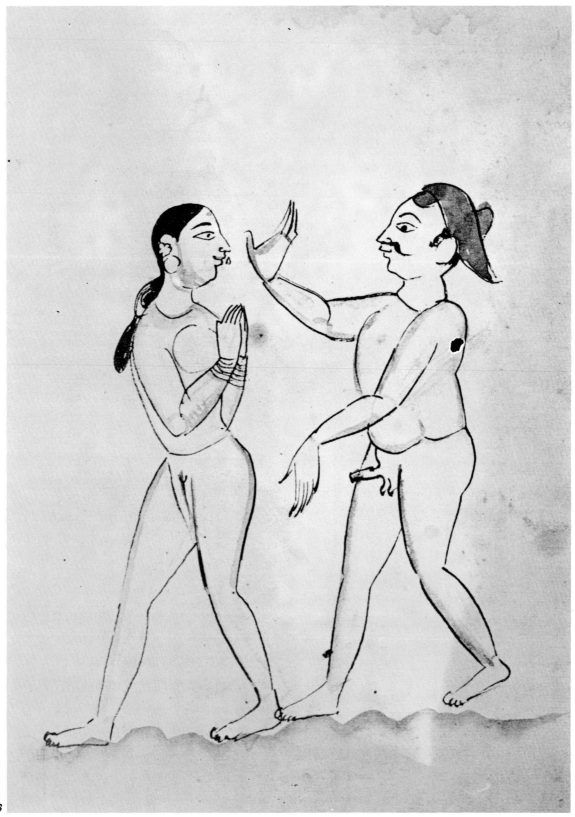

263

186

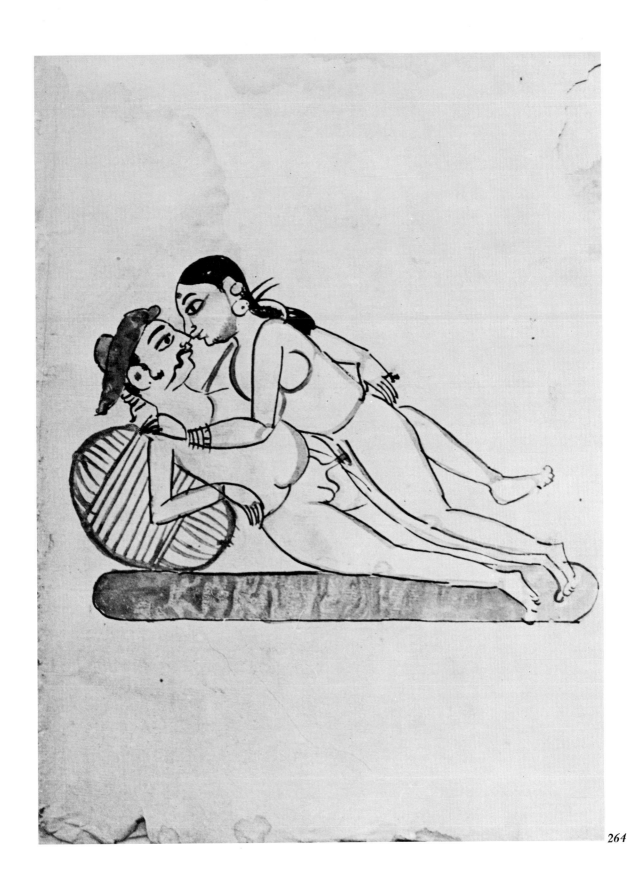

264

263-264—Watercolors, Bengal style, ca. 18th century.

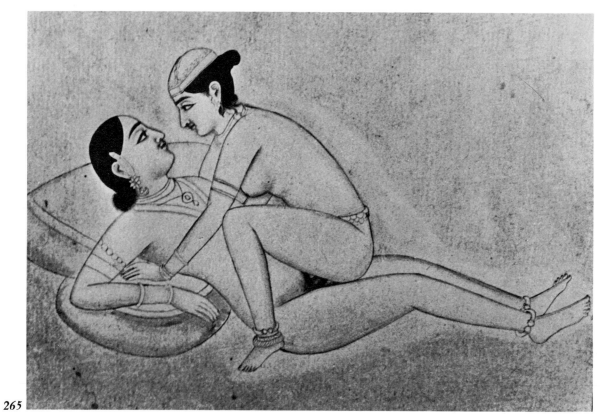

265

266

265—Contemporary pencil and ink drawing. 266—Miniature in delicate watercolors on paper, Central India, mid-19th century.

267   268

267–268—*Two scenes from a painted scroll in brilliant ground pigment colors, late Ming dynasty. (In* Erotic Art, *Vol. I, see Figs. 279–281.)*

269

269–271—Scenes from an unusually wide painted scroll on silk, with rich erotic fantasy and a sense of humor, late-Ming–early-Ch'ing dynasty. (In Erotic Art, *Vol. I, see Figs. 284–285.)*

270

271

272

273

272–273—Scenes from an unusually wide painted scroll on silk, late-Ming–early-Ch'ing dynasty (see also Figs. 269–271).

274

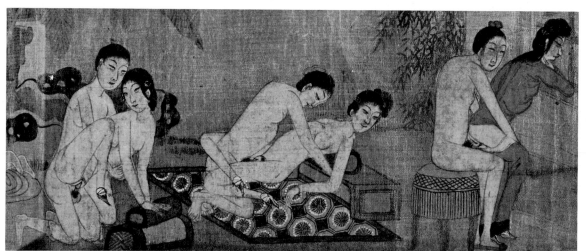

275

276

277

274–276—*Scenes from a painted scroll on silk, late-Ming–early-Ch'ing dynasty. (In* Erotic Art, *Vol. I, see Figs. 282–283.)*
277—*Painting on paper from an erotic album, late-Ming–early-Ch'ing dynasty.*

278

278-279—*Paintings on silk from erotic albums. The pictures in this series are of recent origin. Western influence is evident in the free style and large variety of activities shown. (In* Erotic Art, *Vol. I, see Fig. 304.)*

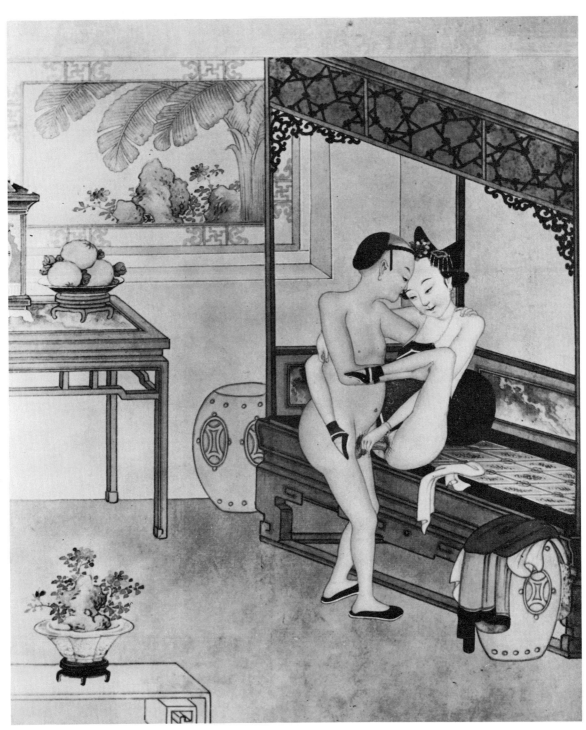

279

280

280–281—*Paintings on silk from recent erotic albums (see also Figs. 278–279).*

283

282–283—*Relatively recent paintings on silk in the classical tradition, though with unmistakable Western influence.*

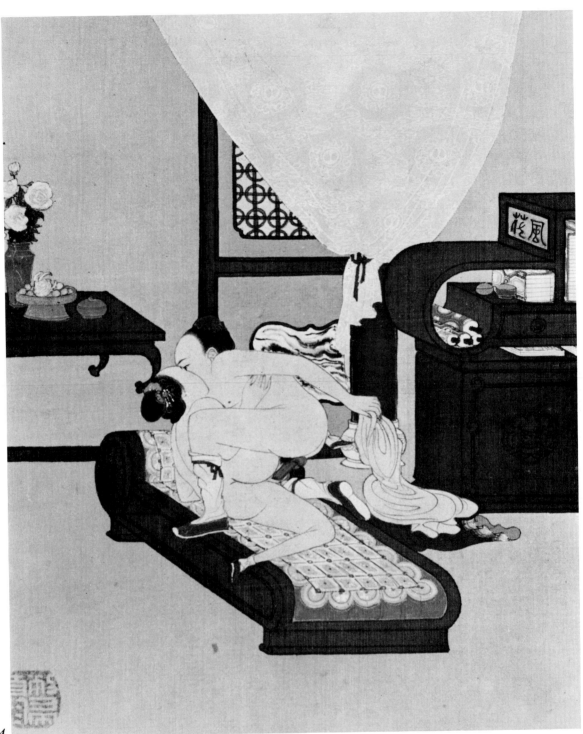

284

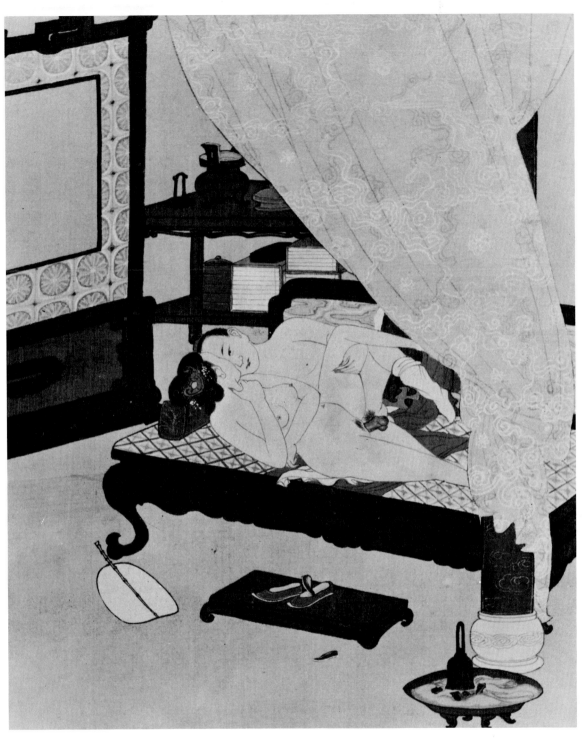

285

284–285—See Fig. 282.

286

287

286–287—See Fig. 282.

288

289

288-289—See Fig. 282.

291

290–291—See Fig. 282.

292

XXXI

XXXII

XXXI and XXXII—*Chinese painted scroll on silk, 18th century.*

XXXIII

شکل هیئت و خیم زن بر کرسی نشسته پای بالا کرده و خرس الیشاد

مجامعت سازد

XXXIV

XXXV

XXXVI

XXXVII

XXXV and XXXVII—*Nakamura Tei-i (Japan), ca. 1930.*
XXXVI—*Rare example of a hanging shunga scroll, early 18th century.*

XXXVIII

XXXIX

XXXVIII and XXXIX—*Japanese painted scroll by Moronobu, early 17th century.*

XL

XL—*Moroshige (Japan), ca. 1690.*

293

292–293—See Fig. 282.

294

294-295—*See Fig. 282.*

295

仇英實父製

296

296–297—*See Fig. 282.*

298

299

298-299—*See Fig. 282.*

300

301

*300—See Fig. 282. 301—Sugimura Jihei, painted scroll (detail),
late 1690's.*

302-303—*Hishikawa Moronobu (1618–1703), woodblock prints, early ukiyo-e school; preceding the development of color woodblock printing.*

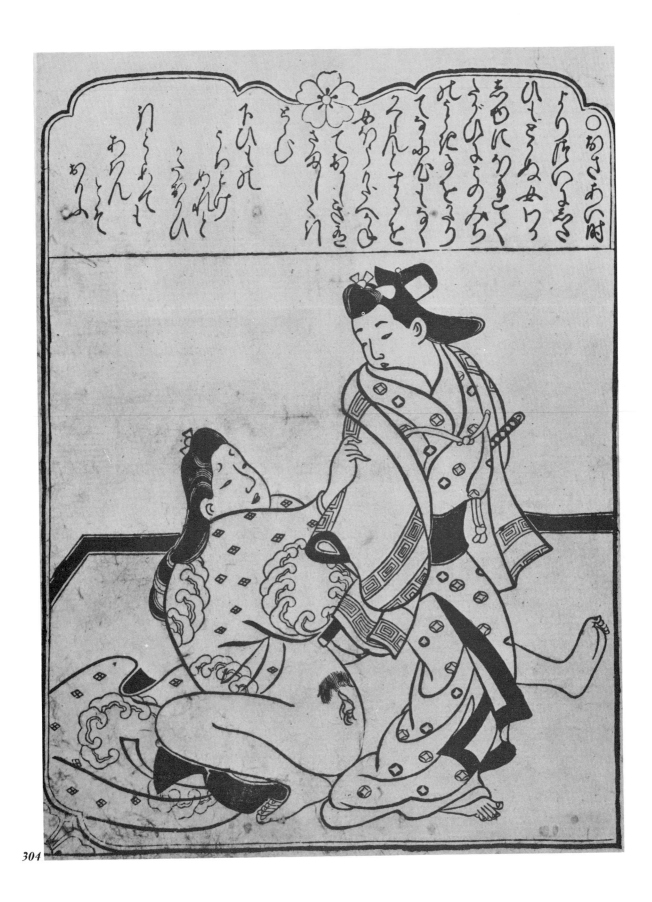

○あさあくのほ
とり屋のよそ
ひしとめぬ女つ
ちやにありもてく
うすひとのかう
れにたすとうら
てうふかしらう
くれんてうと
ありうふくみて
てありさなうくり
らさみくり
らじ

下ひとれ
らわらけ
めれて
うらうひ

けてもらて
ありんとそ
ありえ

304

222

○今いかん
や女らや月
うらうれひうた
してうられ月
のみたうられら
うあらりうろ
のいわれつあ月
りわとうでめら
ゆるあわと
○してうられ
うれたくけく
なりくて
めにうむ
ひのえ
への

てに
さらうで
私わら
かひ
つま

305

306

307

306–307—Masanobu and Nobushige, late 17th to mid-18th century.
308–309—Late 18th to early 19th century, after 16th-century
Yamato-e original.

308

309

310

311

312

313

314

310–311—*Nishikawa Sukenobu (1671–1751), two scenes from painted scrolls.* **312**—*Painted manuscript, style of Sukenobu, 1740's.* **313**—*Colored woodblock print in rare horizontal format, ca. 1820 or earlier, from Osaka school, style of Hokusai.* **314**—*Painting on paper, style of Sukenobu, 1740's.*

315 | 316 | 317

襃姒ジ

幽王

318

315–317—*Maruyama Okyo (1733–95), unusually small painted scroll.* **318**—*Shunchosai, manuscript, 1770's.*

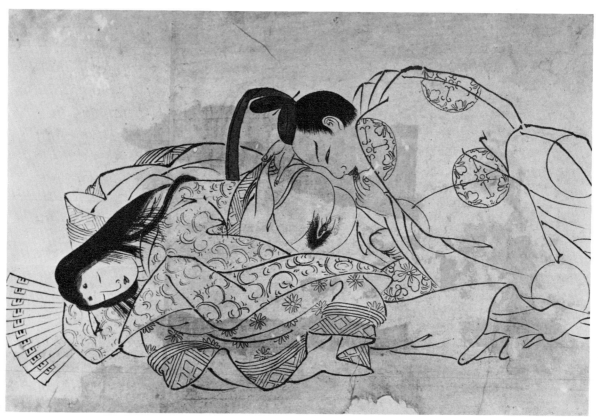

319

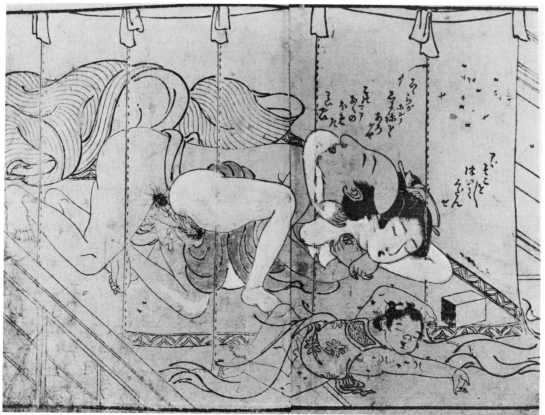

320

321

322

319—*Shunchosai, manuscript, 1770's.* **320**—*Shunchosai, "Thirty-six Poets of the Vagina," woodblock print, 1750's.* **321**—*Katsukawa Shunsho (1726–93), "Festive Scenes," woodblock print, 1780's.* **322**—*Isoda Koryusai (ca. 1770), fine example of 18th-century colored woodblock printing.*

231

323

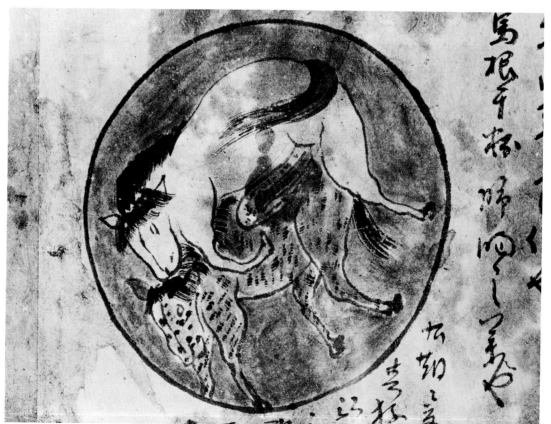

324

325

323—Aoki Mokubei (1767–1833), detail from a scroll version of the famous book Erotic Tales from the East (Daito Keigo).
*324—*Methods of Animal Copulation (Juchiku koketsu-ho), *an early medical treatise on animal copulation and breeding. Dated Kanei, XVII (1640).* 325—*Jichosai, painted scroll, 18th century. Shown is his parody of the "phallic-contest" theme.*

326

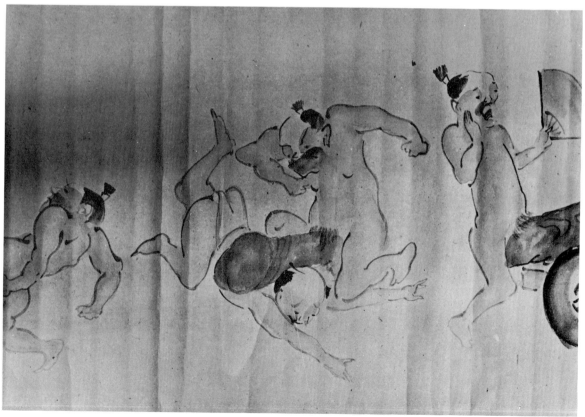

327

328

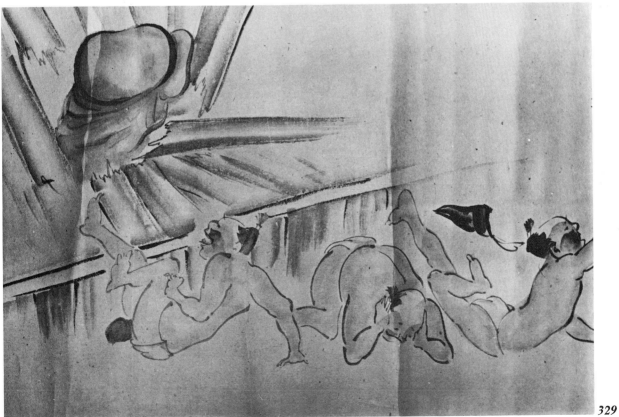

329

326–329—*Jichosai, painted scroll (see Fig. 325).*

330

331

236

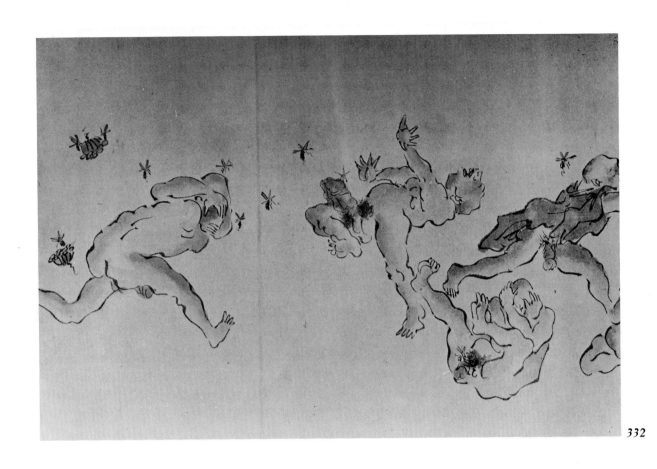

332

330-332—*Shofu Kyosai (1831-89), scenes from his painted scroll, "Blind Men's Fucking Contest."*

333

334

333–334—*Kyosai, two scenes from a painted scroll depicting a record-breaking phallic contest between two groups of courtiers in the old Kyoto Imperial Court. The athletes are with their trainers and sponsors during the measuring contest prior to fighting.*
335—*Utagawa Kuniyoshi (1789–1861), from "Spring Showers," an example of folklore humor, 1850.*

335

239

336

336—*Photo from a contemporary Sumo wrestling match.*
337–338—*Parody of Sumo wrestling, manuscript from late
19th century.*

337

338

339

340

242

341

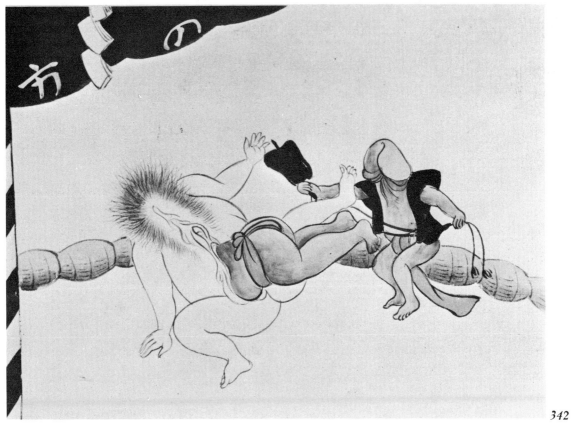

342

339–342—See Fig. 337.

343

344

345

346

343–346—See Fig. 337.

347

348

349

350

347–350—*Paintings on silk, a picture story of the rape of a married woman and her bound and gagged husband's reactions, late 19th century.*

247

351

352

248

353

351–353—*Scenes from a painted album by a modern master (ca. 1930); the album contains seven scenes of sexual sadism under the guise of the 14th-century "Mongol Invasion of Japan."*

354

355

354–357—*Four colored woodblock prints, ca. 1820–60, showing preoccupation with the effect of foreign (Western) influence on Japanese society.*

358

359

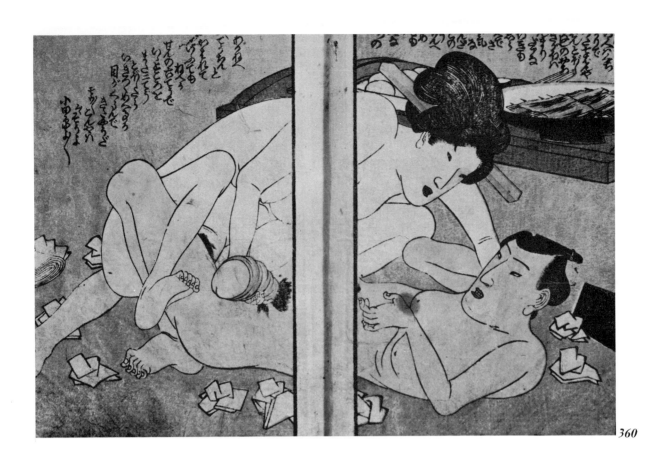

358-359—*Colored woodblock print, early 19th century, Hokusai
school.* **360**—*Sadahide, colored woodblock print, 1830's.*

361

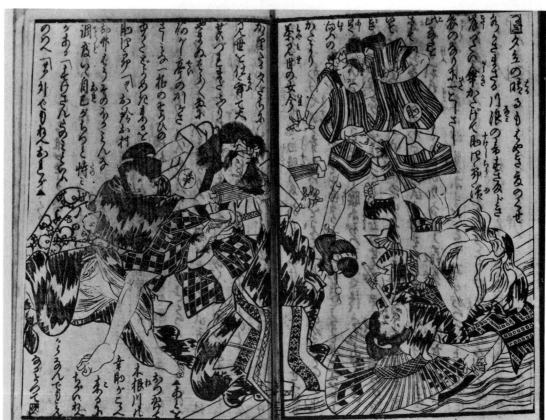

362

363

361—*Yoshikazu, woodblock print (ca. 1845), from* Erotic Life of Hideyoshi. 362—*Keisai Eisen (1791–1848), illustration from* The Doubled Chrisanthemum, *ca. 1840.* 363—*Eisen, colored woodblock print, 1830's.*

365

364—365—*Musume Sotsuyo Shozan, colored woodblock prints, 1850's.*

366

366—Shozan, colored woodblock print, from Yamoto Bunko, *1840's.*

367

367—*Painting on silk, from a manuscript, ca. 1870.* 368—*Page from a vaginal album, paintings in color, ukiyo-e school, ca. mid-19th century.* 369—*From a set of fine colored woodblock prints, showing different types of vaginas, mid-19th century.* 370—*Kunisada, from* Shushoku Bidan, *1840.*

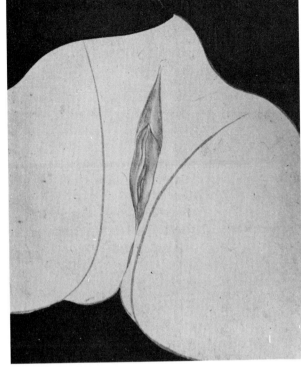

少女洞

第一

方紀十二三

咸之去洞也

洞隙未豐

洞阜未脫

故露見洞

白之隆起洞

俗之嗜嗻

春情未然

又可使然也

368

369

370

371

371-372—*Utagawa Kunisada (1786–1864), colored woodblock prints from* Komon-cho, *early 1860's (see also Fig. 381).*

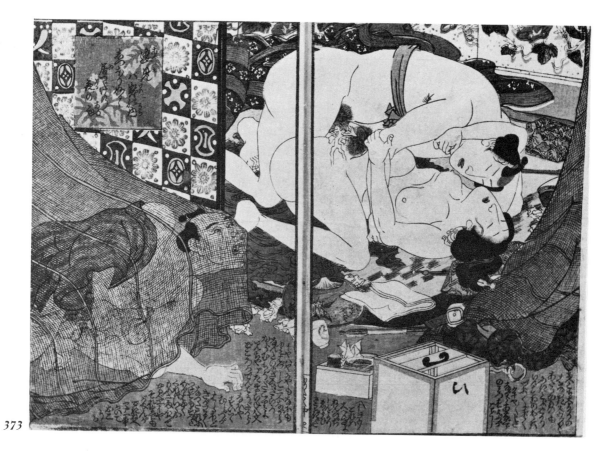

373

374

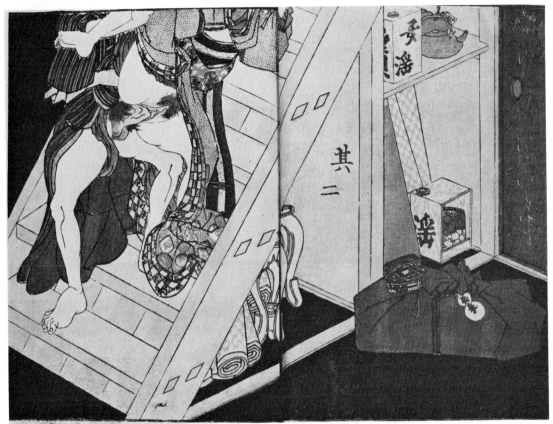

375

376

Kunisada. **373–374**—*Colored woodblock prints from* Tsyu No
Korobine, *1856.* **375**—*Colored woodblock print, 1840's.*
376—*Colored woodblock print from* Views of Edo, *1840's.*

378

Kunisada. *377—Colored woodblock print from* Koi No Urazumi, *1840's.* **378**—*Colored woodblock print, 1860's.*

380

Kunisada. **379**—*From* The Two Butterflies. **380**—*From* Shinkei Bai *(a version of the Chinese* Chin Ping Mei*), 1850.*

381—Kunisada, colored woodblock print from Komon-cho, *early 1860's.*

Index

Index

(In the Index, I refers to the first volume compiled by the Drs. Kronhausen [Erotic Art, Grove Press, N.Y., 1968], while II refers to this volume.)